The Politics
of Reputation

The Politics
of Reputation

The Critical Reception
of Tennessee Williams' Later Plays

Annette J. Saddik

Madison • Teaneck
Fairleigh Dickinson University Press
London: Associated University Presses

Associated University Presses
440 Forsgate Drive
Cranbury, NJ 08512

Associated University Presses
16 Barter Street
London WC1A 2AH, England

Associated University Presses
P.O. Box 338, Port Credit
Mississauga, Ontario
Canada L5G 4L8

The paper used in this publication meets the requirements of the American National Standard for Permanence of Paper for Printed Library Materials Z39.48-1984.

Library of Congress Cataloging-in-Publication Data

Saddik, Annette J., 1966–
　　The politics of reputation : the critical reception of Tennessee Williams' later plays / Annette J. Saddik.
　　　　p.　　cm.
　　Includes bibliographical references and index.
　　ISBN 0-8386-3772-8 (alk. paper)
　　1. Williams, Tennessee, 1911–1983—Criticism and interpretation—History.　2. Criticism—United States—History—20th century. I. Title.
PS3545.I5365Z833　1999
812'.54—dc21
　　　　　　　　　　　　　　　　　　　　　　　　　　　　98-12432
　　　　　　　　　　　　　　　　　　　　　　　　　　　　CIP

For my father, Dr. Meir Saddik
In memory of his wisdom and kindness

Contents

Contents

Preface

In his "intimate memoir" of tennessee williams, dotson Rader describes an incident which occurred in late January 1979 while he was visiting Williams' home in Key West. While Williams himself claimed that he "abhorred the publicity and thought the episode blown out of proportion,"[1] and even went so far as to tell Bruce Smith in 1980 that "that particular event never happened,"[2] Rader's story gives an insight into Williams' general attitude during the later years of his career, and is therefore worth recounting. Rader writes that one night he and Williams were strolling on Duval Street, in a good mood and singing "Southern hymns." They approached five suspicious looking young men who were sitting on the concrete planters on the sidewalk and asked them if they would like to hear a refrain of a hymn. Without waiting for an answer, Williams and Rader began to sing loudly, much to the chagrin of the knife-wielding youths, who surrounded them in a threatening manner. At this point Rader exclaimed that they should run away; Williams, however, "was not about to run":

> "Let's go, Tenn!" I pleaded, grabbing his arm.
> He jerked his arm away, giving me a look of withering contempt for my cowardice. And then he turned his attention to the chief bruiser.
> "My name is Tennessee Williams!" he declared, "and I am not in the habit of retreat!"
> Whereupon they hit *me!*
> After knocking me to the ground, they slugged Tennessee, picked him up, threw him on top of me, and gave me some swift kicks in the side for good measure. They fled down the street, and it was over.
> Later, when I asked him if he had any idea who the bastards were who jumped us, he said, "Baby, they were probably New York drama critics!"[3]

This is how Tennessee Williams perceived his relationship with the drama critics in 1979. Williams had a reputation for sometimes being paranoid, especially in the later years of his career, but in this case he was not entirely wrong in his impressions. Between 1945 and 1961 Tennessee Williams had a total of eleven plays

9

produced on Broadway, and virtually all these productions were successful to some degree, delighting audiences and receiving enthusiastic critical receptions along with numerous awards. After *The Night of the Iguana* (1961), however, no Williams play was to win any major award or experience any significant measure of popular or critical acclaim. Yet since Williams was "not in the habit of retreat," he stood his ground against the (often hostile) reactions of both audiences and critics to his later plays and continued to write diligently and prolifically until his death in 1983. In his biography of Williams, Donald Spoto describes the critics' reactions to Williams' later work despite the playwright's persistent efforts:

> From 1970 to the end of his life, Tennessee Williams continued to work at his craft with his habitual, insistent energy—daily, and sometimes on more than one play, story and poem simultaneously. Only rarely, however, was the result satisfactory to him, to audiences, or to critics. Tennessee Williams was mentioned as the great American playwright whose creative powers went into decline after 1969.[4]

Elia Kazan wrote of Williams that "the last years of his life were pitted with public failures, one disaster following hard on another. But he never stopped writing—and offering his chin for the knockout."[5]

The 1960s were to prove difficult for Williams not only in terms of his work, but in his personal life as well. After the death in 1963 of Frank Merlo, his lover of nearly fifteen years, Williams' use of drugs and alcohol increased to dangerous levels as he plunged into a deep depression. His depression was increased by the fact that he was experiencing one critical failure after another, and his chemical dependency took a toll on both his health and his work:

> I had suffered a great loss in my life . . . and I sought oblivion through drugs. I lived from 1963 to 1969 under various drugs, and while I continued to write every morning, through the use of "speed" injections, amphetamines, intramuscularly, I was not in a very real world and unconsciously I might have been seeking death. . . . I went on speed, and my mind started going too fast for the typewriter.[6]

In 1969 Williams suffered what was apparently a nervous breakdown and was hospitalized for three months in the psychiatric division of Barnes Hospital in St. Louis. Although he was treated for drug and alcohol abuse and felt that he was regaining control of his life in the 1970s, the conventional wisdom regarding the failure of Williams' plays throughout the 1960s and beyond is that his drug-crazed mind was incapable of sustaining his former creative powers. According to Louis Auchincloss, for example, Williams "never captured his old stature" after 1969 because of "a lack of coherent thinking that wrought havoc with [his] later theatre," and a "sentimentality that ultimately broke through walls unsupported by any basic moral fabric."[7]

The purpose of this study of Williams' career is to examine the conventional wisdom regarding it in order to determine whether there are other, more valid, explanations for the failure of his later plays. In doing so, I shall be concerned with the nature of these plays in comparative relation to his early successes and with the assumptions and predilections of the critics who have created the conventional wisdom. During the 1960s Williams claimed that he was deliberately moving away from what the critical establishment saw as the essentially realistic dramatic forms that had established his career to what Lillian Hellman called "the theater of the imagination"[8]—a more antirealistic, fragmented type of drama characteristic of the new movements of the time. He insisted that the negative critical reception of his later work was a result of the critics' failure to set aside their "fixed image" of him as a realistic playwright[9] and evaluate the later plays on their own terms. He felt that the deliberate changes from his early work to the later work in terms of style and presentation were disturbing to the majority of critics, and that their nostalgia for a play such as The Glass Menagerie was preventing them from understanding and/or accepting his later experiments with language and dramatic form. Arthur Ganz has called several of Williams' later plays "rambling discourses with little or no movement toward a climax,"[10] but Williams repeatedly insisted throughout his later years that he was striving for new forms and that the "reviewers were intolerant of [his] attempt to write in a freer way."[11] I believe that Williams' impression of the critics' position is worthy of serious consideration.

Offering a new reading of Tennessee Williams' entire career, I challenge the conventional wisdom that his later work represents a failure of his creative powers. This study especially researches the later career (from 1961 to 1983) and argues that Williams deserves a central place in American experimental drama. By reading through the criticism and comparing the style of this later work with the work of experimental dramatists such as Samuel Beckett, Harold Pinter, and Edward Albee who were shifting the boundaries of dramatic presentation, I demonstrate that what has been characterized as a failure is actually a conscious departure from the early dramaturgy that had established Williams' reputation. The expectations of both the popular and academic press in this country, however, prevented them from accepting Williams' departure from the traditional, more commercial plays presented on Broadway (and made into Hollywood films), which often only flirted with antirealistic devices, to the minimalistic explorations of language, character, and action that challenged realistic presentation altogether.

In chapter one, in order to determine what the critical reception of Williams' work may itself reveal concerning possible reasons for the rejection of his later plays, I document this reception from his first major commercial and critical success, the Chicago production of *The Glass Menagerie* in 1944, to the failures of the 1960s, 1970s, and 1980s. In addition to documenting the reaction of popular reviewers, i.e., those writing mainly for the newspapers immediately after a performance, I examine the reception of Williams' work by a second group of critics whose members were mainly affiliated with weekly and monthly periodicals as well as academic journals. This distinction will serve in establishing whether there existed divergent levels of enthusiasm for Williams' work among his critics according to differing affiliations and venues.

Chapter two focuses on the major works of the early, successful years and examines their nature, which I argue is essentially realistic in form, in their subject of representation, and in the presentation of language, despite Williams' well-known mistrust of realism and his consequent use of antirealistic devices. I discuss *The Glass Menagerie* (1945), *A Streetcar Named Desire* (1947), and *Cat on a Hot Tin Roof* (1955) as examples of the early plays that critics and audiences praised for their narrative consistencies, effective characterizations, and poetic language. Yet while I argue that these early plays embraced the codes of realism, especially when compared to the more experimental later works, I do address Williams' resistance to formal realism during the early years of his career. His ambiguous relationship with realism emerged most evidently in his rebellion against its ideological goals, a point which I illustrate through the relationship between realism and industrial capitalism in both the early plays and in the 1956 film *Baby Doll*.

In chapter three I move to a careful discussion of some of Williams' more strikingly antirealistic later plays which were clearly attempts to produce a "different" kind of drama conducive with the experimental atmosphere of the 1960s and 1970s. Using the much revised *The Two-Character Play* (1969, 1973, 1976) along with two of Williams' one-act plays, *I Can't Imagine Tomorrow* (1966, 1970) and *In the Bar of a Tokyo Hotel* (1969, 1970), I show how Williams was experimenting with theatrical conventions and ironic, fragmented language in ways that departed drastically from realistic presentation. In these later works Williams was depending less and less on realism's desire for referential language and conventional plot to express accurately and directly an intangible truth, as he moved from a type of drama which centered on causal narrative structures, a realistic portrayal of character, and long, poetic speeches to more minimalistic forms which undermined orthodox functions of plot and character development and focused on the silences and gaps in language.

Chapter four is devoted to examining the weaker plays of Williams' later period in order to distinguish them from the more sophisticated, focused ones I discuss in chapter three and to acknowledge that their failure with audiences and critics was valid. As he struggled with experimental forms in the later years of his career, Williams inevitably wrote some uneven plays, many of which were poorly structured combinations of realism and various antirealistic dramatic forms such as allegory and surrealism. *The Milk Train Doesn't Stop Here Anymore* (1963, 1964) and *The Red Devil Battery Sign* (1975), for example, lack the strong central action that realism demands while loosely incorporating the antirealistic devices and ironic language that Williams wanted to explore. Williams' disappointment with the failure of his experimental work during the later years often led him to return to realistic forms in such plays as *A Lovely Sunday for Creve Coeur* (1978, 1980) and *Vieux Carré* (1977, 1979), which he hoped would please the critics, but which no longer held any genuine interest for him since he was committed to new dramatic forms. In *A Lovely Sunday for Creve Coeur*, for example, Williams tried to recapture the sentimental realism of *The Glass Menagerie* which critics continuously praised, but he was unable to create the complex characterization, lyrical dialogue, and powerful dramatic tension that marked the earlier play. These later plays, like much of his work after 1961, failed commercially and critically despite Williams' constant revising.

Chapter five returns to a concern with Williams' critical reception and focuses on why the new direction in his later work was neither recognized nor given a favorable evaluation. I compare the establishment of his reputation in the theater with that of contemporary playwrights such as Beckett and Pinter, whose work was an inspiration for Williams' later experimental style. In his later years Williams often hailed Beckett especially as a major playwright whose work he greatly admired.[12] In *The Two-Character Play*, most strikingly, Williams was aiming for a Beckettian kind of drama—drama that focuses on linguistic play and deliberately lays bare notions of the inexpressibility of expression and the contradictions inherent in the concepts of plot and meaning— while simultaneously drawing on his talent for the poetic lyricism so evident in the early plays. Beckett and Pinter, however, succeeded in winning critical acclaim while Williams' similar experiments were rejected as failures. In order to determine more credible and complex reasons for the rejection of Williams' later plays than simply their supposedly inferior quality, I explore how the theater reviewers who created—and then destroyed—Williams' reputation reacted to the work of avant-garde dramatists such as Beckett and Pinter, and how the critics who established the reputations of these antirealistic playwrights felt about Williams' work throughout his career.

This final chapter is not at all intended as a study of the works of Beckett or Pinter, but rather simply as an exploration of their critical reception in this country. My point in chapter five is not to argue the relative merits of Williams' later plays and the plays of his contemporary avant-garde artists, but to illustrate their common dramatic styles and philosophical goals. The fact that it was these very goals that were harshly criticized in Williams' later plays and praised in the works of other writers indicates that their evaluations were often based less on merit than on reputation. My reexamination of Williams' career addresses his frustration throughout the later period that his established reputation as a realistic, rather commercial playwright ultimately worked against him when he chose to depart from the style that had made him famous. Lyle Leverich observes that in the 1960s Williams

> became acutely aware that he was in competition with himself—the self he had created as Tennessee Williams. He was confronted with what everyone had come to regard as "a Tennessee Williams play," and in the midst of a radically changing theatre, he found himself cut off and in danger of becoming an anachronism.[13]

While Williams' substance abuse during the later years of his career did inevitably affect his writing at times, many of the later works in which he continued to have faith despite brutal negative criticism do, upon close examination, possess the intricate structures and complex language worthy of the creator of *The Glass Menagerie* and *A Streetcar Named Desire*. Moreover, the issues involved in the establishment of Williams' reputation reveal significant insights about the crucial influence of the critics' position on the lasting power of a work, especially in the theater.

Acknowledgments

WHILE BLANCHE DUBOIS MAY HAVE DEPENDED ON THE "KINDNESS of strangers," the completion of this project could not have been possible without my dependence on the kindness of my colleagues, friends, and family who encouraged me throughout its many stages.

To Thomas Van Laan, who has been an invaluable source of guidance, I owe a debt I can never repay for his careful attention, thoughtful comments, and persistent faith in me. My colleagues Elin Diamond and George Kearns have likewise added immeasurably to this project through the wisdom of their insights.

I am also grateful to many who have helped in various ways with the preparation of this book. I thank my friends and former teachers, Michael Shafer and Peter J. Swales, for the early inspiration and love of scholarship they instilled in me long ago; Michael McKeon, Lois Gordon, Patricia Tobin, Marjorie Howes, Bruce Robbins, Cassandra Pappas, and Jennifer Bernstein, for much helpful advice; and, of course, the editorial and production staffs of Fairleigh Dickinson University Press and Associated University Presses, particularly Christine Retz, Michael Koy, Harry Keyishian, and Julien Yoseloff for their support and patience in answering my seemingly endless queries.

To my dear friends who were closest to me throughout the many stages of this project, I owe a heartfelt debt of gratitude: Kathleen Hobbs, for providing much stimulating conversation and keeping me sane with her wit and understanding; Lee Bernstein and Walid Younes, for late-night discussions at the diner and many years of valuable friendship; and Andre Stipanovic, whose affection and companionship guided me through the early stages of this research.

Special thanks are due to a very special man, Richard Thoma, for sharing his creativity with me through the irreplaceable portrait of Tennessee Williams which I will always cherish, for hunting down Williams memorabilia and photographing his residences throughout the country, and most of all, for his unwavering love and support of me and my work. To my ongoing

17

surprise, he not only tolerates my obsession with Tennessee Williams, but continues to encourage it.

The greatest debt of gratitude falls to my family: my sister, Orly Saddik, for her unequaled friendship and for acting out scenes of *A Streetcar Named Desire* with me when we were growing up; my father, Dr. Meir Saddik, for his warmth, inspiration, and the eternal magic his spirit brings to me everyday; and my mother, Gila Saddik, whose wisdom, courage, and beauty keeps me strong. With their love and encouragement, they always made sure I had whatever I needed to grow and learn.

The Politics
of Reputation

1

The Rise and Fall of a Reputation

"[Critics] can praise to high heavens an inferior work and make absolutely merciless ridicule of something much superior. So, how can you possibly predict which way they are going to jump. Sometimes it seems quite arbitrary."
—Williams, interview with Cecil Brown, 1974

By THE TIME HE WAS FIFTY YEARS OLD IN 1961, TENNESSEE WILliams had earned an international reputation as "America's greatest living playwright," boasting four Drama Critics' Circle awards, three Donaldson awards, one "Tony," and two Pulitzer Prizes. His first major success, *The Glass Menagerie,* opened on Broadway in 1945 after it was received enthusiastically in Chicago, and ran for over sixteen months. It was followed by *A Streetcar Named Desire* in 1947, which dominated Broadway for over two years and secured Williams' reputation in the theater. Hollywood immediately capitalized on that reputation and released the film version of *The Glass Menagerie* in 1950 and of *A Streetcar Named Desire* in 1951.

Ten years after *The Glass Menagerie* launched Williams' career, *Cat on a Hot Tin Roof* ensured his continuing fame, enjoying a run of approximately twenty months on Broadway. Acclaim for Williams' work was so enthusiastic by the 1950s that even the minor off-Broadway production of *Suddenly Last Summer* was as successful with audiences and critics as if it had in fact been presented on Broadway. Commercially successful films were eventually made of all the major plays of Williams' early years, including *Cat on a Hot Tin Roof, Suddenly Last Summer, Summer and Smoke, The Rose Tattoo, Sweet Bird of Youth,* and *The Night of the Iguana.* These films were released as major productions starring some of the most famous names in Hollywood: Elizabeth Taylor, Ava Gardner, Geraldine Page, Anna Magnani, Richard Burton, Montgomery Clift, and Paul Newman.

None of Williams' later works ever achieved the success that the early works had. The later plays were, with few exceptions, viewed by audiences and critics as inferior to his earlier accomplishments. While Williams was very prolific in the 1960s, 1970s, and 1980s, the main products of these later years—*The Milk Train Doesn't Stop Here Anymore, Kingdom of Earth* (also known as *The Seven Descents of Myrtle*), *The Two-Character Play* (also called *Out Cry*), *In the Bar of a Tokyo Hotel, Small Craft Warnings, The Red Devil Battery Sign, Vieux Carré, A Lovely Sunday for Creve Coeur, Clothes for a Summer Hotel,* and *Something Cloudy, Something Clear*—often closed after only a few performances, and it was not uncommon for audience members to walk out on these productions. Some of these plays had Broadway openings, but more and more they were produced in small playhouses off-Broadway, off-off-Broadway, and in cities other than New York. A total of fifteen films of Tennessee Williams' works were made, but only two of them came from his later work: *Boom!*, a version of *The Milk Train Doesn't Stop Here Anymore,* and *Last of the Mobile Hot Shots* (known as *Blood Kin* in Europe), a version of *Kingdom of Earth.* Even though *Boom!* starred Elizabeth Taylor, Richard Burton, and Noel Coward, and *Last of the Mobile Hot Shots* starred Lynn Redgrave and James Coburn, neither film achieved any measure of success.

Only a few of Williams' later plays managed to make it to Broadway, and all were failures. *The Milk Train Doesn't Stop Here Anymore* was presented in several versions and had two Broadway runs; the first lasted for only sixty-nine performances and the second for only five.[1] The 1973 New York production of *The Two-Character Play* closed after twelve performances after failing in London and Chicago. *The Seven Descents of Myrtle* closed after approximately three weeks, and *Vieux Carré* after only four days. And in 1980, *Clothes for a Summer Hotel*, Williams' last work to have a Broadway opening, closed after less than three weeks.

The most successful play of the later period was *Small Craft Warnings*, which opened off-off-Broadway in 1972. When the play moved uptown to the New Theatre, Williams entered his own play in the role of the alcoholic doctor to boost ticket sales. Although he didn't take his role seriously, addressing the audience and disorienting the cast by improvising his lines, audiences enjoyed the spectacle. Williams himself, rather than his work, was becoming the main attraction. But even with Williams' appearance in the play, *Small Craft Warnings* only managed a run of over three months.

The success or failure of Williams' offerings at the box office throughout his career was, of course, dependent upon the critical response to his plays, and therefore the critical evaluation of Williams' work needs to be carefully considered in documenting its overall reception. In doing so I shall be drawing on a distinction which John Gassner makes in his book *The Theatre in Our Times*, where he distinguishes between the work of two types of theater critics—the popular "reviewer" and the more serious intellectual "critic." For Gassner,

The reviewer—in so far as he can be distinguished from the critic—will submit to the spell of the production, if it is an effective one. He is more susceptible, so to speak, to the conspiracy of playwrights, director, actors, and others to put the play "across" on the stage. Moreover, he *should* be susceptible, even when he carries his faculty of judgement with him; otherwise he will be a stick of wood in an audience full of live people.[2]

By contrast, he writes,

The critic's function is, of course, to discover whether the play is artistically solvent, . . . [it] is not that of an agent of the theatre whose business it is to make a play succeed. His business is to evaluate or judge the work rather than put it "across." He is a detached, disinterested party in this respect.[3]

Robert Brustein, in *Seasons of Discontent*, a collection of his theater reviews, cites Williams' own distinction between the "mass audience" and the "intellectuals." Williams writes: "I want to reach a mass audience. I feel it can dig what I have to say, perhaps better than a lot of intellectuals can. I'm not an intellectual."[4] Brustein uses this comment to express his own distinction between serious and popular evaluations of art. Brustein defines the group that Williams calls the "intellectuals" as "that smaller group which demands that his art be uncompromisingly honest."[5] He sees Broadway's "mass audience," on the other hand, as a source of "easy admiration" for the playwright, and describes this group condescendingly as "the mink matrons and the expense account executives."[6]

Unlike reviewers such as Brooks Atkinson, Walter Kerr, and Harold Clurman, who were mainly affiliated with the popular press, critics such as John Gassner, Robert Brustein, Eric Bentley, and Kenneth Tynan had intellectual affiliations and venues as well as more specific academic ties. These critics were typically associated with weekly and monthly periodicals as well as academic journals. Eric Bentley, for example, served as the drama critic to *The New Republic* from 1952 to 1956, and Robert Brustein joined the magazine in 1959. John Gassner, who ultimately secured the position of Professor at Yale University, had been one of the youngest members of the Drama Critics' Circle in the 1950s and had also been Williams' drama teacher at the New School in New York City. These critics often collected their reviews to be published as books. Gassner notes in the preface to *The Theatre in Our Times* that the book was "essentially a collection of essays new and old, although much revised; and the latter originally appeared in publications as diverse as *The Atlantic Monthly, Theatre Arts, The Forum, The Quarterly Journal of Speech, The Educational Theatre Journal,* and *Theatre Time.*"[7] He does not specifically state which of his reviews or articles appeared in which publication, or even if specific information is new to the book or has been previously published, but the list of periodicals above indicates the venues for his writing during his career. Kenneth Tynan was associated with several British and American publications throughout his prolific career—*The Observer, Encounter, The New Yorker,* and *The Atlantic,* to name only a few.

Rather than turning out newspaper reviews for members of a mass audience who were interested in finding out whether or not they would enjoy a play, the critics were writing for a more "intellectual" audience who sought to carefully examine the subtleties of a work and evaluate it according to their own set of prescribed standards. It is the close examination of a work after careful reflection over time that the critics feel it is their duty to present, as opposed to the immediate enthusiasm that the reviewers may be seduced into expressing shortly after seeing a performance. While the distinction between "reviewers" and "critics" is obviously not one of conviction and finality, it is nonetheless one which holds up in general and is well worth making in considering the evaluation of Williams' oeuvre. I borrow these terms from Gassner throughout my discussion in order to draw attention to the divergent expectations and even prejudices that were imposed upon Williams' work by the critical community according to each group's sense of purpose, associations, and ideological investments.

During the early years of Williams' career the reviewers in general responded very favorably to his work. Among reviewers, there was no doubt that Williams' contribution to the world of drama was salient and enduring. Even some of Williams' early

Broadway productions that were not immediate and unqualified successes with audiences and critics managed to gain ultimately some measure of acclaim. Although his major Broadway offering of 1948, *Summer and Smoke,* was not very well received and closed after less than three months, a reworked version of the play was presented off-Broadway in 1952 and became a great success, running to capacity audiences for almost a year.[8] Similarly, while *The Rose Tattoo* opened on Broadway to "decidedly mixed"[9] reviews in 1951,[10] it was nonetheless awarded the "Tony" for best play, and ran for almost nine months. Both *Summer and Smoke* and *The Rose Tattoo* were eventually considered major works of the Williams canon, succeeding with mass audiences and, for the most part, with reviewers.

Williams credits two Chicago reviewers, Claudia Cassidy of the *Chicago Daily Tribune,* and Ashton Stevens of the *Herald American,* with giving him his "start in a fashion . . . with *Menagerie* in '44."[11] Cassidy said that the play had "the stamina of success. . . . [It] knows people and how they tick. . . . If it is your play, as it is mine, it reaches out . . . and you are caught in its spell."[12] And Stevens wrote that *Menagerie* "has the courage of true poetry couched in colloquial prose."[13] The New York reviewers agreed with their colleagues in Chicago. Lewis Nichols, writing in the *New York Times,* reviewed the New York production very favorably:

> Preceded by warm and tender reports from Chicago, "The Glass Menagerie" opened at the Playhouse on Saturday, and immediately it was clear that for once the advance notes were not in error. Tennessee Williams' simple play forms the framework for some of the finest acting to be seen in many a day. . . . [The play] combines qualities of humor and human understanding.[14]

Similarly, George Jean Nathan said that *The Glass Menagerie* "provides by long odds the most imaginative evening that the stage has offered this season."[15]

A major supporter of Williams' plays from the beginning of Williams' career, Brooks Atkinson of the *New York Times,* also praised *The Glass Menagerie* highly, calling it Williams' most perceptive creation and claiming it had "pity for people, coolness of perspective, poetic grace, and forbearance."[16] In 1947, while *A Streetcar Named Desire* was experiencing "a storm of critical acclaim,"[17] Atkinson wrote a rave review of the play for the *New York Times.* He called *Streetcar* "By common consent, the finest new play on the boards."[18] In 1955 Atkinson described *Cat on a*

Hot Tin Roof as a "stunning drama" and wrote that the play "is the work of a mature observer of men and women and a gifted craftsman."[19] Walter Kerr was another major reviewer who enthusiastically supported Williams' early work. In a review of *The Rose Tattoo* for *The Commonweal* on 23 February 1951, Kerr wrote that Williams was "the finest playwright now working in the American theatre."[20] Kerr's 1958 review of *Suddenly Last Summer* also praised Williams, complimenting his "spare, sure, sharply vivid control of language" and calling the play "a serious and accomplished work."[21]

In 1957 Harold Clurman hailed Williams as one of the most "outstanding playwrights of recent years,"[22] and on 9 March 1962, *Time* magazine put Williams on its cover and devoted a lengthy article to his life's work and outstanding achievements. *Time* hailed *The Night of the Iguana* as "a box office sellout and much the best new American play of the season" and asserted that "The fact is that Tennessee Williams . . . is a consummate master of theater. . . . He is the greatest U.S. playwright since Eugene O'Neill."[23]

Time's celebration of Williams' talent reflected the reviewers' enthusiastic support overall during the early years of his career, as the reviews cited above are typical of the acclaim that Williams' work experienced up to and including *The Night of the Iguana*. After that, however, the reviewers found it difficult to say anything positive about his later plays. Their overall reaction was confusion, dismay, and the sense that Williams' work had become too personal and self-pitying.

When *The Two-Character Play* was produced in London in 1967, the reviewers were "baffled." W. A. Darlington said in the *Daily Telegraph* that he "could make no sense of [it] and long before the end had stopped trying to." In the *Daily Express*, Herbert Kretzmer said that "It would need a psychoanalyst—and preferably Tennessee William's [*sic*] own—to offer a rational intrepretation [*sic*] of the enigmas that litter the stage like pieces of an elaborate jigsaw." And Peter Lewis of the *Daily Mail* said the play had "technique without content—or at least content obscured and muddled by sheer technique."[24]

But the New York reviewers were often the most brutal. Clive Barnes opened his review of *The Seven Descents of Myrtle* with the complaint that "Time was when Tennessee Williams wrote plays, but now he seems to prefer to write characters." The rest of his review neither overtly praises nor condemns *Myrtle*, but he calls the play (and its title) "mysterious," and claims that he is "relieved to note that Mr. Williams has already received a $400,000 down payment on film rights."[25] In his review of Williams' next play, *In the Bar of a Tokyo Hotel*, Clive Barnes began somewhat comically (and bitterly):

> After I reviewed Tennessee Williams's last play [*Myrtle*] his agent sent me a telegram of complaint. Now, having last night at the Eastside Playhouse seen Mr. Williams's latest play, "In the Bar of a Tokyo Hotel," I feel like sending *her* a telegram of complaint.[26]

Barnes goes on to say that "The play seems too personal," and that "more pity and less self would be a distinct advantage."

Even Walter Kerr was no longer as supportive of Williams as he had been. After the 1977 opening of *Vieux Carré* on Broadway, Kerr's review in the *New York Times* was typical of the play's general reception. Although he still believed that Williams was "our best playwright," he felt that *Vieux Carré* was simply a series of "aimless" dream images and echoes with "no dynamic pattern . . . to house them," rather than a coherent and focused drama.[27] Later, in a 1980 *New York Times* review of *Clothes For a Summer Hotel*, Kerr, while continuing to defend Williams and insist that he was "the finest playwright of our time," lamented that

> The most dismaying thing about Tennessee Williams's pursuit of the poor, sad ghosts of Scott and Zelda Fitzgerald, "Clothes for a Summer Hotel," is the fact that Mr. Williams's personal voice is nowhere to be heard in it. It is as though the playwright's decision to deal with actual people—not only the Fitzgeralds but Ernest Hemingway and the Gerald Murphys as well—had momentarily robbed him of his own imaginative powers.[28]

Kerr ends his review by noting "the absence of the author's inimitable flair for language" and says that "'Clothes for a Summer Hotel' is Tennessee Williams holding his tongue."

There were, however, some individual exceptions to the dominant opinion that Williams' later plays were disappointing failures. For example, in 1967 the reviewer of the *Times* of London, David Wade, found the London production of *The Two-Character Play* to be insightful, writing that "Mr. Williams succeeds quite brilliantly in sustaining the idea that nothing whatever is to be relied upon and that if we get through one veil there is just another beyond."[29] Lawrence Van Gelder called the New York 1975 production of *The Two-Character Play* "Demonic, ghost-ridden, elliptical," and said that the play

> endures—and it appeals. Not to all tastes, not for all times, and certainly not because it bears the name of a distinguished playwright. It endures because of the assurance of its craftsmanship, and it appeals because it plays to what bedevils us all—fear.[30]

Yet these positive reactions were clearly exceptions to the general opinion of Williams' later plays, and even these few exceptions were usually qualified ones. Clive Barnes, while condemning *In the Bar of a Tokyo Hotel* as a failure, did acknowledge that there were some strong moments in the play. He wrote that even though "the play repelled [him] with its self-pity, . . . there are plaintive notes of poetry recalling Williams at his very best."[31] Bruce Smith writes that "On an optimistic note," Clive Barnes believed that "*Tokyo Bar* is avant garde and will be appreciated in the theatre of the future."[32] Richard Eder, reviewing *A Lovely Sunday for Creve Coeur* in 1979, said that the characters were not convincing, that "they seem to be in disguise." Eder did, however, feel the play had "humor, soft-edged irony and a virtuoso command of theatrical complexity" and that it was "full of virtues." Overall, he concluded that *A Lovely Sunday for Creve Coeur* had "many of the elements of a fine play, but not a central one."[33]

Reviewers have often linked the failure of Williams' later work with his abuse of drugs and alcohol, which accelerated after the death of his lover, Frank Merlo, in 1963, and apparently led to a nervous breakdown in 1969. C. W. E. Bigsby aptly sums up the general impression regarding Williams' personal and artistic situation during the 1960s:

> The 1960s were to prove a personal and artistic debacle [for Williams]. His dependence on drink and drugs led him to the mental hospital and to the violent ward . . . The plays that he produced . . . were often brutal, apocalyptic and death-centered. He frequently came close to self-parody, a kind of narcissism which reflected his paranoia and self-concern. His talent fed off itself and the effect was a series of shrill, neurotic appeals having to do with the intolerable pressures which threaten to destroy the sensitive, the poetic, the betrayed.[34]

Spoto claims that by 1964 Williams' depression and substance abuse led him to become virtually a recluse, and that after his breakdown Williams' "body was wounded, his mind was ravaged, his spirit had been shattered—by the death of Frank Merlo, to be sure, but just as violently by chemicals. It would be naive to pretend that this confluence did not affect his art."[35]

After spending the 1960s (a period he often referred to as his "stoned age") under the influence of various narcotics, Williams began to feel that he was recovering control of his creative powers. The reviewers, however, did not feel this way. The plays that Williams presented in the 1970s and 1980s were not received any more warmly than his failures of the 1960s. In fact, it seems that by the 1970s the reviewers had essentially given up on Williams altogether, expecting him to fail.

The estimations of Williams' early work by the critics were more ambivalent than those by the reviewers, as they expressed the opinion that Williams' work was *almost* great, but not quite. The critics tended to praise Williams as a dramatist during the early years of his career, but with qualifications. They never shared the pure enthusiasm for Williams' work that the reviewers had, and from the beginning of his career saw Williams as mainly a commercial playwright rather than a serious writer of enduring literature. John Gassner praised Williams' early work, stating that "His portraits of women who cannot face reality are masterful."[36] Yet Gassner qualifies his praise, feeling that Williams' "'estheticism,' which has made him unusual and fascinating in the American theatre, has been his main limitation as a dramatist . . . ever since I started following his career in 1940."[37] While hailing *A Streetcar Named Desire* as the best play of the 1947–48 season,[38] Gassner complained of its "ambiguities," and claimed that Williams had "reduced the potential tragedy [of *Streetcar*] to psychopathology."[39] Overall, his evaluation of the play was itself ambivalent:

> *Streetcar,* for all its dramatic momentum and surge, is a divided work. Ambiguities split the emphasis between realistic and decadent drama, between normal causation and accident, between tragedy and melodrama. Although *Streetcar* crackles with dramatic fire, it lacks a steady flame. Its illumination flickers.[40]

Gassner also maintained that "Enthusiasm for . . . *The Rose Tattoo*—or even *A Streetcar Named Desire*—. . . can be greatly modified upon more or less close examination."[41] Eric Bentley's evaluation of Williams' early work closely mirrored that of Gassner, combining cautious initial enthusiasm with detailed complaints. Bentley praised *Streetcar* in *Harper's Magazine* as a new play "worth mentioning,"[42] and said that "Tennessee Williams stands head and shoulders above Haines, Miller, and Stavis."[43] Yet, like Gassner, Bentley qualifies his praise, claiming that "*A Streetcar Named Desire* seems to me on the *borderline* of really good drama."[44] He goes on:

> If [*Streetcar*] is never safely across the border, it is because . . . the sentimental patterns are at work which cramp most honest effort in the theater today. Perhaps we are not sure how limited, how small, Williams's play is until the last scene. But in realistic and psychological work the last scene is a test case. We look there to find the answer to the question: How deep does the play go? The episode of the black-coated couple from the madhouse compels the answer: not very.[45]

Bentley even goes so far as to say in *The Dramatic Event* that "it is arguable" that *Streetcar* would have failed without the artistic "changes" of Elia Kazan.[46]

In evaluating *Cat on a Hot Tin Roof* for *The New Republic*, Bentley wrote that "There is no one in the English-speaking theatre today who can outdo Mr. Williams' dialogue at its best: it is supple, sinuous, hard-hitting . . ."[47] Yet again, he felt the need to qualify his praise of Williams' play:

> If some things in Mr. Williams' story are too vaguely defined, others are defined in a manner far too summary and definite. The characters, for example, are pushed around by an obsessively and mechanically sexual interpretation of life.[48]

Bentley called Big Daddy Williams' "best male character to date,"[49] yet felt that "Not all the characters are credible"[50] and that "something is terribly wrong. To say there is no unity of effect is the understatement of the century."[51]

Kenneth Tynan also tended to be ambivalent in his overall evaluation of Williams' talent. Writing for *The Observer* in 1954 Tynan called Tennessee Williams one of "the prose masters of the contemporary English-speaking theatre"[52] and said that Williams, along with Arthur Miller, has "produced the most powerful body of dramatic prose in modern English."[53] Yet while Tynan singled out *The Glass Menagerie* as a "great example" of the genre of the "memory play" in 1958, he was not ready to call it a major work.[54] In 1954 he claimed that "The play is not a major achievement,

but its opacity is as precise and marvellous as a spider's web."[55]
His attitude toward *Cat on a Hot Tin Roof* was similarly undecided:

> *Cat on a Hot Tin Roof* was eighteen months in the writing. I now think
> it is [Williams'] best work, but when I first saw it, it struck me as an
> edifice somehow tilted, like a giant architectural folly. It was august,
> all right, and turbulent, but there were moments of unaccountable
> wrongness, as if a kazoo had intruded into a string quartet.[56]

Tynan, however, did not blame Williams for the "moments of
unaccountable wrongness"; instead, he blamed Elia Kazan. Tynan felt that Kazan's (in)famous revision of the third act harmed
rather than helped the play, and he advised Williams that "a less
creative collaborator might, in the long run, be more helpful."[57]

Tynan's reaction to Williams' next major work after *Cat, Suddenly Last Summer*, was not ambivalent. He called the play an
"excursion to the brink of paranoia," and suggested that "we
must pray for Mr. Williams' return to the true dramatic world of
light and shade, where the easy violence of melodrama is soft-
ened by compassion."[58] Tynan's attitude toward *Summer and
Smoke* was negative as well. In 1954 he wrote that *Summer and
Smoke*, "a needlessly symbolic morality play, is sentimental in that
its characters are too slight to sustain the consuming emotions
which are bestowed on them."[59]

Robert Brustein followed the trend of the other critics in his
estimation of Williams' early work. In the late 1970s he wrote
that "Tennessee Williams has been the most celebrated postwar
American dramatist, and the strongest influence on the American
realist theatre."[60] In 1973 he lamented in the *New York Times* that
"Certainly, there is little evidence on Broadway these days of any
interest in relevant American myths of the kind that . . . informed
the shattering conflicts of Williams' *A Streetcar Named Desire*."[61]
Yet this is the extent of his praise. In 1962 he wrote of *The Night
of the Iguana* that

> Tennessee Williams has composed a little nocturnal mood music for
> muted strings, beautifully performed by some superb instrumental-
> ists, but much too aimless, leisurely, and formless to satisfy the atten-
> tive ear. . . . *The Night of the Iguana* enjoys no organizing principle
> whatsoever; and except for some perfunctory gestures toward the
> end, it is very short on plot, pattern, or theme.[62]

Those critics who were even more fully defined by their association with the academic community, being affiliated mainly with

universities and academic journals, had much the same reaction as the other critics. For example, Signi Falk—the author of one of the earliest books on Tennessee Williams (for the Twayne series in 1961) and a professor at Coe College during that time—wrote in *Modern Drama* in 1958 that

> Tennessee Williams has been called "an artist to the fingertips," "a master of sensitive characterization," a writer with "hypnotic quali-ties," of "exquisite tastes," and "the foremost new playwright to have appeared on the American scene in a decade." And yet, the fact that many critics . . . have given the highest praise to the acting and the production, raises the question of whether the quality of the play-wright's work has not been obscured by brilliant productions.[63]

Falk calls Williams a "sentimentalist who fluctuates like a ther-mometer in uncertain weather between bathos and poetic rheto-ric, between the precious and the bawdy, and between adolescent admirations and histrionic displays of violence."[64] She concludes her essay with the overall evaluation that "Even though [Wil-liams'] plays leave much to be desired, the actors, directors and the producers have been able to make of his scripts exciting eve-nings in the theater."[65]

Some essays on Williams' work from the critics were entirely favorable, but their praise tended to isolate aspects of Williams' talent: most typically his poetic language, evocation of "mood," or construction of character. Robert Emmet Jones, for example, writing in *Modern Drama* in 1959, wrote a very flattering essay on Williams' early heroines, saying that

> Critics have generally agreed that the heroines of Tennessee Williams are his finest creations. They dominate the plays in which they are found, and to them, as representatives of certain Southern types, Williams has brought much insight. This insight, which is at once poetic and sociological, has, since 1945, provided the American the-ater with several characters who may well rank in future histories of American dramatic literature with Eugene O'Neill's Anna Christie and Nina Leeds as the most successful creations of dramatic heroines in the first half of the twentieth century.[66]

When it came to Williams' later work, however, the reaction of the critics closely reflected that of the reviewers. No longer ambivalent, the critics increasingly rejected the later plays. Robert Brustein's reaction to *The Milk Train Doesn't Stop Here Anymore* was typical. He ends his very brief 1963 review of *Milk Train* with a dismissal of the play, claiming that

> the writing is soft, the theme banal, the action sketchy, the play un-finished—and since there is no drama, why should there be a review, especially when the directing, the decor, and the acting (except for a sharp portrait of a Capri witch by Mildred Dunnock) are as indifferent as the text?[67]

Brustein's overall evaluation of Williams' later career is that at some point "Williams stopped trying to be an artist."[68]

Arthur Ganz, writing in the *American Scholar* in 1962, called *A Streetcar Named Desire, Summer and Smoke, Cat on a Hot Tin Roof,* and *Suddenly Last Summer* "remarkable."[69] But he had a different opinion of Williams' later work. In an updated version of his article for his 1980 book *Realms of the Self,* Ganz retains the 1962 observation of the early work, but dismisses Williams' later plays in general as having an "absence of conflict":[70]

> The most obviously personal, and even self-indulgent, of these late plays is *Out Cry.* . . . Even less appealing is the distracted artist of *In the Bar of a Tokyo Hotel,* whose madness makes him the easy victim of his cruelly vital wife, herself a victim of passing time. This contrast between inert pathos and comparative vitality, regularly presented through pairs of women in the later works (Celeste and Trinket in *The Mutilated,* the Molly-Polly figures and the Fraulein in *Gnadiges Fraulein,* Leona and Violet in *Small Craft Warnings*), runs through Wil-liams's other plays of the late 1960s and early 1970s. But whereas this motif was handled with evocative complexity in Williams's earlier work (Amanda and Laura, Stanley and Blanche,Maggie and Brick are the most obvious examples), here everything is awash in a flood of sentimentality that invites, though it cannot induce, sympathy for the suffering victims.[71]

"Personal," "self-indulgent," and "sentimental"—like the review-ers' evaluation of Williams' work, these adjectives are typical of the critics' evaluation in the later years of his career. William J. Free (writing in 1977), illustrates that for the second half of Wil-liams' career both reviewers and critics were essentially of the same mind. Drawing on the responses of both these groups, he states that "Critical dissatisfaction over Tennessee Williams' plays of the seventies has been almost unanimous,"[72] and that "Critics of *Out Cry* have complained specifically about the overwhelming triteness of the dialogue and the personal subjectivity of the dra-matic images."[73]

Since the critics were, for the most part, either ambivalent or blatantly disparaging toward Williams' work throughout his career, it was clearly the reviewers who essentially built his outstanding early reputation in this country and abroad. However, while the plays Williams presented during the early period of his career were almost all unanimously successful with audiences and with the reviewers, there were a few exceptions. After a preview run in Philadelphia, *Sweet Bird of Youth* was presented on Broadway in 1959 and was, like Williams' other early plays, "a great commercial success."[74] Yet while Smith claims the play opened to "rave reviews,"[75] it seems that although some reviewers responded favorably to the play, many were decidedly unsatisfied with Williams' latest work, feeling that he had gone too far with his indulgence in sordid subjects. Brooks Atkinson, still responding favorably to Williams' work, but becoming more lukewarm in his support, called *Sweet Bird* "a portrait of corruption and evil" and "hardly a noble play," but granted that "it has overtones of pity for those who are damned." While he ultimately felt that *Sweet Bird* was "acrid," he did believe that Williams was "in a relaxed mood as a writer," and asserted that "As a writer of prose drama, Mr. Williams has the genius of a poet."[76] Harold Clurman wrote that *Sweet Bird* interested him "more as a phenomenon than as a play. . . . Its place in the author's development and its fascination for the audience strike me as more significant than its value as drama,"[77] and John Chapman, while emphasizing Williams' strengths, called him a "dirty minded dramatist who has been losing hope for the human race [and] has written of moral and physical decadence as shockingly as he can."[78] What these critics found objectionable is what they saw as the inherent shock value and essentially negative attitude of a play which deals with the violence of taboo issues such as racism, venereal disease, and castration. Still, paying audiences came to see the play, and *Sweet Bird of Youth*, which ran for almost a year, was considered a successful play by Broadway standards.

In 1960 Williams offered Broadway what it seems to have wanted, Tennessee Williams in a lighter, nonviolent, and less "nihilistic" mode with *Period of Adjustment*. The play "enjoyed some measure of critical success"[79] and closed after 132 performances. Smith writes that "In general, the critical summation was that it was not Tennessee in top form, but all were amazed that he had written what was as close to a light comedy as he could manage."[80] Williams himself never thought much of *Period of Adjustment*; in a letter to Cheryl Crawford (who produced the play) he wrote that "it was not his best work by any standard, but that it was an honest appraisal of how he saw intimate relations; he added that his motive was to earn money for Rose's care."[81] Brooks Atkinson, apparently seeing that the play was not a committed effort on Williams' part, observed that *Period of Adjustment* "is so far below Mr. Williams's standard that it proves nothing one way or the other. His heart is not in that mediocre jest."[82]

The most significant exception to the successful work of Williams' early years was *Camino Real*, a full length play developed out of his 1948 one-act, *Ten Blocks on the Camino Real*. After initial tryouts in New Haven and Philadelphia, *Camino Real* had its Broadway premiere in 1953 and closed after a run of less than eight weeks.[83] While Williams' earlier successful plays had been essentially realistic in form (albeit with a heavy symbolic slant), *Camino Real* was Williams' first full length play that broke with realistic conventions altogether. In another letter to Cheryl Crawford (who went on to produce the play with Ethel Reiner), Williams called *Camino* "an extended poem on the romantic attitude to life."[84]

The reviewers almost unanimously considered the play a disaster. In New Haven and Philadelphia, *Camino* had gotten very bad notices, failing with both reviewers and audiences. Many audience members were outraged by *Camino*'s lack of traditional narrative plot and stormed out of the theater in disgust. In New York, the reviews were generally merciless. Walter Kerr, who respected Williams' work immensely and often declared him America's best playwright, wrote in the *New York Herald-Tribune* that *Camino Real* was "the worst play yet written by the best playwright of his generation. . . . The play is all method—studiously applied—and method applied to a vacuum."[85] In a letter to Williams the following month Kerr offered the playwright what he saw as constructive criticism, insisting that audiences were "outraged by a blank wall, by the play's defiant lack of esthetic clarity." Kerr told Williams that

> What terrifies me about *Camino Real* is not what you want to say but the direction in which you, as an artist, are moving. You're heading toward the cerebral; don't do it. What makes you an artist of the first rank is your intuitive gift for penetrating reality, without junking reality in the process; an intuitive artist starts with the recognizable surface of things and burrows *in*. Don't swap this for the conscious, rational processes of the analyst, the symbolist, the abstract thinker.[86]

Apparently what "terrified" Kerr was Williams' movement away from realistic drama, what Kerr saw as his "junking" of reality. Kerr's comment is indicative of the crux of negative reactions that *Camino Real* received from the press. Kerr acknowledged that Williams was attempting to move in a direction away from realistic drama, yet Kerr didn't support this move. He was convinced that

> The brilliance of Williams' best work lies precisely in its admission of complexity—in Blanche du Bois [sic] tying a noose around her own white throat, in Alma Winemuller [sic] defeating her purposes with every pitiful word she utters—and in the humble acceptance of complexity as the root condition of all our lives.[87]

Kerr's violent reaction to *Camino Real* betrays the kind of drama he valued and the kind of drama he expected from Williams. Like Kerr, reviewers generally felt that "What makes [Williams] an artist of the first rank is [his] intuitive gift for penetrating reality, without junking reality in the process." The failure of *Camino Real* with audiences and reviewers is crucial in the context of Williams' later reception, since it indicates that once Williams began to blatantly move away from the essentially realistic dramaturgy which had made him famous, his following turned against him. Kerr has a single objective standard in mind for judging good drama, defining the "intuitive artist" as one who "starts with the recognizable surface of things and then burrows *in*." This standard seems to have been shared by reviewers in general whenever Williams departed from realistic form. Bruce Smith writes that *Camino Real* was

> so different from Tennessee's almost perfectly Aristotelian creations that audiences had a hard time appreciating it. . . . America seemed to want him firmly in the Aristotelian mode. When he abandoned it, his audiences abandoned him.[88]

By the time of the Broadway failure of *Camino Real* and the qualified critical success of *Sweet Bird of Youth*, it was clear that not only did audiences and reviewers want to see Williams in his "Aristotelian mode," writing essentially realistic plays, they also wanted him to write "delicate" plays that avoided controversial issues and outbursts of extreme violence. The reviewers who had built Williams' reputation were not willing to budge from the pigeonhole that they had created for him and in which they had trapped his image. If they didn't get sensitive realism in the tradition of *The Glass Menagerie* or psychological complexity and dramatic tension à la *A Streetcar Named Desire*, they were sorely disappointed. The criticism *Sweet Bird* received confirmed the reviewers' preference for plays in the spirit of the nonviolent *Menagerie* beyond Williams' other works. In November 1956, a limited run off-Broadway revival of *Menagerie* had "charmed audiences and critics," and "The prevalent critical opinion was that this was the kind of play that Williams should continue to write."[89] John Chapman called *Menagerie* Tennessee Williams' "finest play . . . [an] affectionate, compassionate and poetic nocturne."[90] Even Brooks Atkinson wrote in the *New York Times* in 1956 that

> Although Mr. Williams has written some overwhelming dramas since 1945, he has not written anything so delicate and perceptive [as *Menagerie*]. . . . To see it again is to see how much he has changed. . . . Mr. Williams has never improved on the daintiness and the shy allusiveness of the prose writing in this introductory play.[91]

While some reviewers were able to point out positive aspects of Williams' later plays, the elements they praised continued to betray blatantly the nostalgia for *The Glass Menagerie* that permeated their expectations. For instance, after an essentially unfavorable review in the *New York Times*, Clive Barnes observed of *In the Bar of a Tokyo Hotel* that "Mr. Williams can take heart. There are more flashes of genius here than in any of his later plays . . . [and] there are bursting sharp exchanges of the dialogue that recall "The Glass Menagerie" in their suddenly poignant pertinence."[92] In general, whenever Williams moved away from his earlier dramatic style toward what Kerr described as "the cerebral . . . the conscious, rational processes of the analyst, the symbolist, the abstract thinker,"[93] the overall opinion of the reviewers was that this was not Williams' territory. Both audiences and reviewers clearly did not support Williams' movement towards what he saw as "freer" forms in drama.[94] David Greggory said that after the opening of *The Milk Train Doesn't Stop Here Anymore* in 1963, "people who were expecting *Menagerie* or *Streetcar* were totally confused."[95]

By the end of Williams' career, it undoubtedly took a play in the style and mood of *The Glass Menagerie* to get any sort of favorable reaction from the reviewers at large. The reviews for *A Lovely Sunday for Creve Coeur* (which opened off-Broadway in January 1979) were mixed, and Spoto points out that "several critics in fact praised the gentleness and humor of the play, and welcomed his return, after other wilder experiments, to the traditional form of *A Lovely Sunday for Creve Coeur.*" He goes on to say that the play has a "desperate tone," and that "the lonely women are very like the confused quartet of *The Glass Menagerie.*"[96] Although Spoto's comparison of *Lovely Sunday* and *Menagerie* is reductionistic, the play's superficial resemblance to *Menagerie* in terms of style and mood does follow the pattern of the type of Williams drama that the reviewers were inclined to praise. By 1979, however, mixed reviews were not enough to keep a Tennessee Williams play running, and *A Lovely Sunday for Creve Coeur* closed after only thirty-six performances.

It is important to note at this point that, unlike the reviewers, the critics did not overtly condemn the antirealism of *Camino Real.* Rather, the reaction was, like that toward the earlier plays, ambivalent. In evaluating the play for *The New Republic,* Eric Bentley wrote that although "The genuine element in Tennessee Williams had always seemed to me to reside in his realism,"[97] "*Camino Real* doesn't even pretend to be realism. The unreal which formerly crept up on us [in plays such as *Streetcar*] here meets us head on." Bentley continues:

> Whether New York will prefer this [*Camino's* overtly unrealistic form] I do not know. Possibly the escape into unreality was welcome in the former plays only because it was disguised as its opposite; and now that it is overt the public will either reject it or declare it unintelligible; in which case the play is done for.[98]

Yet it is difficult to get a sense of exactly how Bentley feels about Williams' departure from realistic form. He wrote that "In *Camino Real,* Mr. Williams is not a dramatist but a scenario writer."[99] Bentley decided that he "dislike[d] the script and like[d] the production," but he gave the credit for any positive aspects of the production to Elia Kazan.[100] Kenneth Tynan, however, disagreed with Bentley's evaluation. Tynan felt that

> the published text [of *Camino Real*] has a unity never achieved by the acting script. It carries to its conclusion Williams' dictum: "I say that symbols are nothing but the natural speech of drama."[101]

Overall, Tynan concluded that

> Many charges can be brought against *Camino Real.* It has too many italics, too many exclamation marks; it depends too much on boozed writing and aureate diction. Its virtue is in its affectionate championing of the flyblown, inarticulate stratum of humanity.[102]

These evaluations give us some insight into the type of drama the critics admired, but since they were always suspicious and ambivalent concerning the artistic validity of Williams' work, his ambitious projects were not examined as seriously as they should have been. While the critics were willing to grant that a play like *Camino Real* had its merits, they simply could not see Williams as a dramatist of "ideas." After evaluating *Summer and Smoke* in 1948, John Gassner diagnosed "the weakness I have suspected in the author for some time—an insufficient exertion of intellect."[103] Spoto writes that by the time that *Milk Train* opened in January 1963, "critics like Richard Gilman had been in the vanguard of a new sourness in the business of reviewing." Spoto reports that Gilman

> wrote in *Command* of Williams's "creative suicide," in an article super-ciliously and cruelly titled "Mistuh Williams, He Dead," and he ex-panded his anger for the *Tulane Drama Review* later that year: "The American drama is itself almost mindless; we weep for the intellectual deficiencies of [Arthur] Miller and Williams." A lacerating tone was beginning to infect the writing of a few critics—a callous indifference not only to an artist's past achievements, but also to his present feel-ings. Apparently Miller and Williams were not acceptable to some academics; that they were intellectual deficients creating "mindless drama" was itself a mindless exaggeration.[104]

What most reviewers found objectionable in the case of *Camino Real* was essentially the antirealistic, fragmented style Williams was deliberately exploring. Williams' interest in experimental forms could be seen as early as 1945 with his one-act play, *The Purification*, which he describes in the stage directions as "A play in verse to be performed with a musical accompaniment on the guitar."[105] Although *The Purification* and *Camino Real* are the only radical departures from the essentially realistic plays of Williams' early period, his exploration of antirealistic dramatic forms from the beginning of his career is significant in light of the later plays, since this indicates that the experimental later work exhibits a development of his prior interests rather than a random depar-ture brought about by excessive drug use, as is often argued. In a 1962 interview with Lewis Funke and John E. Booth, Williams discussed his revision process for *The Night of the Iguana*, the play which is generally considered the end of his early, successful pe-riod. Williams' comment exhibits a significant turning point in his thinking about drama, and a desire to work with language in a new way:

> I suddenly saw the light—that there were enough long speeches, which is my specialty, unfortunately, and that at least five or six pages earlier in the act could be reduced to a sort of a dynamic, you know— rather than talk—it would be more effective that way. I realized there was too much talk. I mean there were speeches of five lines where half a line could have done it. Right now I'm engaged in trying to say—trying to express a play more in terms of action. Not in terms of physical action; I mean, in sort of a gunfire dialogue instead of the long speeches that I've always relied on before. Let me say that I depended too much on language—on words.[106]

While Williams' movement from a "depend[ence] on language— on words" to a more minimalistic dialogue does not necessarily indicate a shift away from realism, the fact that he was depending less and less on the ability of discursive language to communicate accurately and completely an idea or emotion—a "truth"—is a movement toward nonrealistic drama, which resists the (realist) assumption that language is able to represent directly an objective reality. Instead, the nonrealistic forms Williams was experiment- ing with in the later plays focus on expressing meaning that can only be articulated through incomplete, fragmented dialogue and the silences which surround it. Leverich feels that in both *The Glass Menagerie* and *The Two-Character Play*, Williams "was con- veying with the power of illusion what in life is so often inexpress- ible: the tragic failure to communicate one's true feelings not only to others but also to oneself in an interior dialogue."[107]

   Throughout his later period Williams often made a point of explaining that he was intentionally departing from realistic drama—that he was striving for new forms. In a 1973 interview Williams claimed that the "reviewers were intolerant of [his] at- tempt to write in a freer way."[108] He then went on to explain what he felt was the problem with the critical reception of his later work:

> They want to try to judge you on traditional form when you're trying to move to something freer, like presentational theater, when you depart from realism and put style on the presentation itself.[109]

In a 1974 interview for *Partisan Review*, Cecil Brown asked Wil- liams about *The Two-Character Play*:

> INT.: What's your opinion about that play now? It was not very well received. The *New York Times* was bothered by the lack of humor and

the hermaphroditic nature of the two characters, feeling that this two-character play was actually a one-character boring monologue.

WILLIAMS: I think it's my best play since *Streetcar Named Desire*. But they (critics) don't understand it, but they will one day.

INT.: What does it have that your other plays do not? What's so great about it?

WILLIAMS: It's a very personal play. It's my own human outcry. The style is different too.[110]

Williams' insistence that *The Two-Character Play* was "different" in style and that the "critics" simply "didn't understand it" was an opinion he was to hold until his death.

In 1979 Williams said that New York reviewers have a "fixed image of you—which is usually hostile—in their minds when they go to see your work."[111] Williams' drama of the 1980s tried once again to move away from that "fixed image" and convince the reviewers that he was moving on to newer forms in drama. *Clothes for a Summer Hotel* was one such attempt. Smith felt that, like the situation with *Camino Real*, *Clothes for a Summer Hotel* "escaped adequate appreciation," since America seemed to want Tennessee Williams "firmly in the Aristotelian mode."[112] When Williams approached Elliot Martin, the producer of *Clothes*, to discuss casting of the play, Williams insisted that he was not writing the same kind of dramas as he had done earlier in his career, much to the chagrin of the reviewers. Martin remembers Williams' words:

"I want to warn you, Elliot," he said to me, "the critics are out to get me. You'll see how vicious they are. They make comparisons with my earlier work, but I'm writing differently now."[113]

The reviewers' general objection to changes in Williams' choice of dramatic mode or subject matter since his first Broadway success was to be detrimental to Williams throughout his career, but most prominently in his later years, when these deliberate changes in terms of style and presentation were most extreme.

2

"I Don't Like to Write Realistically": Williams' Uneasy Relationship with Realism

"I want people to think 'This is life.'"
—Tennessee Williams on *Cat on a Hot Tin Roof*

MOST OF WILLIAMS' MAJOR DRAMATIC SUCCESSES OF THE 1940S and 1950s—the plays which were well-received by both the public and the reviewers—made use of an essentially realistic mode of representation, despite some nondiegetic devices he may have used for ultimately realistic purposes, such as the emphasis of what he called central "truths" (as in *The Glass Menagerie*) or the reinforcement of a distinction between reality and fantasy (as in *A Streetcar Named Desire*).[1] Yet Williams' ambivalence concerning realism as it was currently typical during the 1940s and 1950s is well documented. This ambivalence emerged in his early works as a subtle challenging of the boundaries of realistic presentation, both in his dramaturgy (the abundant use of nondiegetic devices) and, more importantly, in his undermining of realism's ideological goals. Therefore, a central complexity of Williams' early work lies in its ideological rebellion against realism while simultaneously working within its boundaries.

Because of this complexity, there has, throughout the years, been some debate on the issue of whether many of the early plays do in fact fall under the heading of realism. John Gassner writes that "the most affecting scenes of *The Glass Menagerie* are written with sensitive realism. . . . In his best scenes and plays . . . Williams has managed realism without excess and with considerable insight, sympathy, and accurate observation."[2] Ronald Hayman asserts that "Except for *Camino Real*, all Williams's major plays" before *The Milk Train Doesn't Stop Here Anymore* (1963) "had been realistic,"[3] and Bruce Smith considers the plays Williams wrote during the early, successful phase of his career to be "almost perfectly Aristotelian creations,"[4] presumably in their achievement of the identification, catharsis, and unity of action which realism embraces.

By contrast, others see Williams' early plays as either deliberately avoiding realism or, at the very least, not entirely embracing it. C. W. E. Bigsby claims that "Williams was never interested in realism,"[5] and Benjamin Nelson writes that

> Williams does not pretend to be a realist. None of his plays are realistic in a strict sense of the word and some are protests against realism. (Note the highly unrealistic settings for *The Glass Menagerie* and *Cat on a Hot Tin Roof*.) But these plays have at their core the solid bone of shrewd realistic observation by a playwright and thinker who is well aware of the facets of the human condition.[6]

Joseph N. Riddel argues that "To see *A Streetcar Named Desire* as a realistic slice-of-life is to mistake its ambitious theme" since, "just as in *The Glass Menagerie*," Williams is "groping for a . . . universal statement" and aspiring "to say something about man and his civilization."[7] In *In Search of Theatre*, Eric Bentley describes *A Streetcar Named Desire* as "rather realistic," but fails to elaborate on the reason for this qualifier. He goes on to call *Streetcar* a "well composed play of American life which seem[s] more realistic than it is . . . [since] the actors are handled in the 'Stanislavsky' manner, and the action is domestic drama with lots of punch and personal emotion."[8]

The debate over whether Williams wrote realistic plays during the early years of his career is, to a certain extent, a result of the imprecision of the label *realism*, and the above quotations emphasize the ambiguity involved in employing such a label. Nelson, for example, sees the settings of *Menagerie* and *Cat* as so "highly unrealistic" that for him they practically invalidate the "realistic observation" at the core of these plays, and Riddel limits realism to a "slice-of-life" presentation which is apparently not conducive to an "ambitious theme." For Bentley, *Streetcar*'s realism rests on its acting style, action, and its use of identification/catharsis ("personal emotion"), but for reasons unexplored he still feels the need to qualify his evaluation of the play as realistic. The lack of consensus in determining a specific understanding of realism is, of course, due to the overlapping implications and fluid boundaries associated with literary forms, genres, and labels. Like all such labels, realism is a slippery term and needs to be defined before it is applied. The dichotomy of "realistic" and—on the other end of this simplified critical spectrum—"antirealistic," "nonrealistic," or "experimental" drama, will aid me in distinguishing between a kind of dramaturgy that, for the most part, embraces essential principles drawn from realistic assumptions, and dramaturgies that, in some major way, react against realism's mode of representation. In employing these terms I do not wish to give the impression that I am creating a fixed and stable dichotomy that exists in the absolute. Nor do I wish to assert that Williams' early plays are quintessential examples of realistic drama, since such a statement would, of course, reduce the complexity of his dramaturgical subtleties. Rather, I seek only a discourse which acknowledges the dramaturgical changes evident throughout Williams' career and which will allow me to discuss some of the reasons for those changes. While the limitations of such a discourse are obvious, it will help me draw a distinction between the dominant style of Williams' early, successful plays, and the "different" kind of drama he presented in his later years—a distinction necessary to exploring his development as a dramatist and the critical reaction to his work.

Realism as a literary form aims to represent directly abstract truths by making reference to the codes that society uses to construct and identify the real. Improbabilities and stylistic effects are rejected in favor of a more faithful representation of "life and the social world as it seems to the common reader, evoking the sense that [a text's] characters might in fact exist, and that such things might well happen."[9] A central illusion of realism is objectivity, telling the "truth" or representing the world externally "as it really is," as opposed to the subjectivity of individual or psychological experience. Moreover, there is a disclosure of "truth" and an element of closure associated with realistic fiction, a return to order following a series of challenges to that order. Catherine Belsey writes that realism

> is characterized by *illusionism*, narrative which leads to *closure*, and a *hierarchy of discourses* which establishes the "truth" of the story. . . . But the story moves inevitably towards *closure* which is also disclosure, the dissolution of enigma through the reestablishment of order, recognizable as a reinstatement or a development of the order which is understood to have preceded the events of the story itself.[10]

The restoration of a dominant order that Belsey addresses is crucial to realistic fiction, which is always profoundly ideological in its presentation of the real. Rather than simply presenting mutable versions of reality, realism sets up representation as unassailable truth—the "mirroring" of an objective world and of a fixed "human nature." Vivian M. Patraka writes that "the seamless unity of realism conceals the history of its own making, thereby suggesting that all the events which are depicted occur naturally and inevitably,"[11] and Elin Diamond asserts that "Realism is more than an interpretation of reality passing as reality; it *produces* 'reality' by positioning its spectator to recognize and verify its truths."[12]

Ian Watt argues that, in fiction, formal realism is "the narrative embodiment of a premise . . . or primary convention" that the novel

> is a full and authentic report of human experience, and is therefore under an obligation to satisfy its reader with such details of the story as the individuality of the actors concerned, the particulars of the times and places of their actions, details which are presented through a more largely referential use of language than is common in other literary forms.[13]

George Levine also attempts to locate and define realism—that "inescapable word"—despite the fact that it is a "dangerously multivalent one." Levine concludes that "Whatever else [realism] means, it always implies an attempt to use language to get beyond language, to discover some non-verbal truth out there."[14] While Watt and Levine are discussing realism in terms of its emergence during the rise of the eighteenth-century *novel*, their descriptions certainly pertain to the establishment of realistic conventions and language in drama during the nineteenth century. Dramatic realism sought to rid theatrical representation of the "artificiality" that characterized early nineteenth-century dramaturgy, and is usually defined as a

> movement in the theatre at the end of the 19th century which replaced the well-made play and the declamatory acting of the period by dramas which approximated in speech and situation to the social and domestic problems of everyday life, played by actors who spoke and moved naturally against scenery which reproduced with fidelity the usual surroundings of the people they represented.[15]

Realism as a dramatic form seeks to represent "faithfully" a "slice-of-life" and maintain the "fourth-wall" illusion that the members of the audience are, in a sense, eavesdroppers and voyeurs, witnesses to events in the "real lives" of the characters assembled on stage. In accordance with this, the audience of an essentially realistic play is rarely, if ever, directly addressed, and grandiose or "artificial" linguistic patterns tend to be avoided in favor of an attempt to reproduce language the audience can recognize as its own. Works of realism aim to investigate social and material conditions, referring to prevailing social mores and values, as well as the dress, speech patterns, and means of interaction contemporary with their audiences. Overall, dramatic realism seeks to naturalize the relationship between stage presentation and outside world, suggesting that the representation is the real.

While it may be true that "Williams was never *interested in* realism,"[16] his early successes are generally realistic in terms of the kind of action which takes place, the way language is used, and the way in which both the visible and invisible environment is defined. Levine's description of realistic fiction can be applied to Williams' early plays such as *The Glass Menagerie* (1944), *A Streetcar Named Desire* (1947), and *Cat on a Hot Tin Roof* (1955), as these works can certainly be seen as "self-conscious effort[s] . . . in the name of some moral enterprise of truth telling and extending the limits of human sympathy, to make literature appear to be describing directly not some other language but reality itself."[17] Williams' dramaturgy was also aiming for the Aristotelian notions of dramatic action, identification, and catharsis in his earlier plays, central goals of realism against which much antirealistic drama rebelled. In 1959 he wrote that

> if there is any truth in the Aristotelian idea that violence is purged by its poetic representation on stage, then it may be that my cycle of violent plays have had a moral justification after all.[18]

In an essay entitled "The World I Live In" for the *London Observer* (7 April 1957), Williams wrote of his themes and his characters ("individuals") in realistic, even naturalistic, terms. Naturalism has often been seen as an extension of realism in its desire to achieve an even more "scientific" and therefore accurate representation of life and human beings existing in the order of nature. Essentially a product of post-Darwinian biology of the nineteenth century, naturalism claims that character and behavior are entirely determined by the forces of heredity and environment. Williams' emphasis on "uncomprehended influences" and "circumstance" in his early plays clearly indicates a naturalistic treatment of theme and character:

> I don't believe in "original sin." I don't believe in "guilt." I don't believe in villains or heroes only right or wrong ways that individuals have taken, not by choice but by necessity or by certain still uncomprehended influences in themselves, their circumstances, and their antecedents.[19]

Like realism, naturalism in the theater seeks to overthrow conventions of the classical and romantic traditions that, as Zola believed and asserted in *Naturalism in the Theatre* (1881), "were based on the rearrangement and systematic amputation of the truth."[20] Instead, naturalism favors a more faithful portrayal of human beings trying to live in "our present environment,"[21] as "the physiological man in our modern works is asking more and more compellingly to be determined by his setting, by the environment that produced him."[22] Zola called for a rejection of conventional "theatre language," a language he saw as a stylized version of the author's own, which is uniformly "put into the mouths of all . . . characters, men, women, children, old folk, both sexes and all ages" alike.[23] He insisted that in naturalistic theater characters must "speak as you do in everyday life"[24] since "to create living people you must give them to the public not merely in accurate dress and in the environments that have made them what they are, but with their individual ways of thinking and expressing themselves."[25]

When Joseph N. Riddel argued that *Streetcar* is not a realistic slice-of-life drama simply because it possesses an "ambitious theme," the implication, of course, is that ambitious themes are incompatible with realism.[26] Riddel's assumption has no basis, especially since realism's desire to directly represent truth is certainly ambitious. In a letter to Elia Kazan concerning the production of *A Streetcar Named Desire*, Williams speaks of an actual objective truth which can (and should) be expressed in art:

> [I]n creative fiction and drama, if the aim is fidelity, people are shown as we never *see* them in life but as they *are*. Quite impartially without any ego flaws in the eye of the beholder. We see from the *outside* what could not be seen *within* and the truth of the tragic dilemma becomes apparent. It was not that one person was bad or good, one right or wrong but that all judged falsely concerning each other. What seemed black to me and white to the other is actually

gray—a perception that could occur only through the detached eye of art. As if a ghost sat over the affairs of men and made a true record of them.[27]

Williams' view of the "detached eye of art," which gives an "impartial" and "true" record of human affairs, is a realist view, and one which the dramaturgy of his early plays attempts to express.

From the beginning of his career, however, Williams was clearly uncomfortable with a strict formal realism, and therefore his early plays made use of some expressionistic and symbolic devices, giving his realism a "twist." John Gassner writes that "Williams . . . has been suspicious of realism, no doubt because he has seen so much degenerate realism in the form of commonplace playwriting."[28] Gassner discusses Williams' "concern with nonrealistic formal devices" and claims that "Williams' fondness for atmospheric and musical effects is transparent, and his consciousness of dramatic and theatrical form makes him a deliberately 'theatricalist' playwright":[29]

> Williams' work has been popularly called "poetic realism." It edges over into *theatricalist realism* because he tends toward the symbolist school of writing, and whenever symbolism has to be given physical equivalents it becomes theatricalism. Had he devoted himself solely to poetry he would have been a "symbolist." Fortunately he did not, for he would have been a distinctly minor, perhaps only barely tolerable, lyric poet. The theatre has compelled him to objectify experience, which he can do very well.[30]

Williams' voiced distrust of the "commonplace" realism of his day coupled with the nondiegetic devices such as "music [which] comes out of nowhere [and] lighting [which] is symbolic"[31] have been central reasons for some critics seeing his early plays as antirealistic. In *Streetcar,* the haunting music of the "Varsouviana," the polka which was playing the night Blanche's young husband Allan shot himself, "sounds . . . in a minor key faint with distance" whenever she recalls that traumatic evening (1:355, 381), while the lighting of the sky "invests the scene with a kind of lyricism and gracefully attenuates the atmosphere of decay" (1:243). Similarly, Williams uses music in *Menagerie* "to give emotional emphasis to suitable passages" and notes that the lighting "is not realistic" since it bears "a certain correspondence to light in religious paintings" (1:133–34).

In his production notes to *The Glass Menagerie,* Williams writes:

> Expressionism and all other unconventional techniques in drama have only one valid aim, and that is a closer approach to truth. When a

play employs unconventional techniques, it is not, or certainly shouldn't be, trying to escape its responsibility of dealing with reality, or interpreting experience, but is actually or should be attempting to find a closer approach, a more penetrating and vivid expression of things as they are. The straight realistic play with its genuine Frigidaire and authentic ice-cubes, its characters who speak exactly as its audience speaks, corresponds to the academic landscape and has the same virtue of a photographic likeness. Everyone should know nowadays the unimportance of the photographic in art: that truth, life, or reality is an organic thing which the poetic imagination can represent or suggest, in essence, only through transformation, through changing into other forms than those which were merely present in appearance. (1:131)

We can see in this passage that, early on, Williams desired to reject what he saw as the "photographic" aspects of realism—the emphasis on resemblances to familiar surfaces. Rather, he was aiming for a "closer approach" to truth which exists beyond the superficial. However, although he sought to get beyond surfaces—to find "a more penetrating and vivid expression of things as they are"—he still assumed that a nonverbal essential "truth, life, or reality" could be represented through the "poetic imagination." The mode he chose for representing or expressing that "poetic imagination" in his most famous early plays was largely through a dramaturgy which embraced Aristotelian principles, but which did not seek simply to reproduce the referential codes of reality, such as icecubes and Frigidaires. Gassner's concept of "theatricalist realism" is much closer to the dramaturgy of Williams early plays than is the frivolous dramatic realism (prevalent in theater and film at the time) that Williams flatly rejected as "unimportant." Williams manipulated formal realism in order to create a particular dramaturgy which *included* realism's "surfaces"—settings meant to represent the contemporary social environment and the objects in it, as well as how subjects in this environment look, dress, behave, and interact—but he added to this certain devices that were not strictly realistic in a literal sense, yet were employed with the purpose of representing the "truth" he was after more fully. In other words, Williams' mode of representation and his central aim in the early plays—the representation of objective "truth"—were essentially conducive with realistic principles, even though he rejected the "degenerate realism" of his day and often made use of nonrealistic devices in achieving that aim.

The most immediate access to a playwright's dramaturgy is through language, especially when dealing primarily with the written text rather than with particular productions which would, of course, incorporate tone, action, and mise-en-scène in their performances. The directness of articulation and the familiar images which language constructs makes it the primary mode for representing or expressing truth in realistic drama, and in Williams' case, especially, language takes center stage with dialogue presented in the poetic style that has become the trademark of his early plays. The language of Williams' early plays is heavily dependent on symbolism and exhibits a greater degree of lyricism and overdetermination than is normally present in common speech. Williams believed that "plays can be just as lyrical as a poem can be; you can use just as much personal lyricism in a play as you can in a poem."[32] Williams' language is therefore a major part of his dramaturgy, and the fact that it is presented in an essentially realistic manner—largely referential and intending to represent the actual speech (however "poetic") of characters who portray contemporary human beings—is a central reason for identifying his early plays as realistic. The "poetry" of Williams' dialogue aids—rather than undermines—his realistic purpose of articulating a truth which exists beyond surfaces.

Williams' main problem with realism during the early years rested on his sense that the dramaturgy dominating the conventional brand of realistic theater, with its overemphasis on a "genuine Frigidaire and authentic ice-cubes," was inadequate for his "conception of a new, plastic theatre" which must take its place (production notes to *Menagerie*, 1:131). He believed that drama *could* in fact represent reality, but that the superficial dramatic forms that had degenerated from classic realism had become so conventional that they were not the best way to express that reality. In the production notes to *Menagerie*, Williams rejects a dramaturgy he feels provides inadequate access to truth in favor of a fresher and therefore more *accurate* one. Yet while Williams was struggling to avoid what he saw as the tired conventions of realism in his early years, it is undeniable that his early work simultaneously embraced the conventions of realism in its search for "a closer approach" to representing "things as they are."

In his very useful 1992 study of Arthur Miller and Tennessee Williams, *Communists, Cowboys, and Queers*, David Savran points to Williams' production notes for *The Glass Menagerie* where, he states, "Williams writes approvingly of the use of 'expressionism and all other unconventional techniques' on the stage." Savran argues that

> Most critics have taken Williams at his word and have granted a priority to the one "unconventional technique" he specifies: expressionism. Thus, Mary Ann Corrigan, for example, classifies Williams as a kind of expressionist manqué and then proceeds to describe all of Williams's nonrealistic devices as expressionistic (while never providing a definition of expressionism that differentiates it from the other modernist avant-garde movements).[33]

Savran objects to this classification by Corrigan and others of Williams' work as expressionist on the grounds that

> Williams's plays insistently challenge the expressionist model . . . for the simple reason that none of them stages the psychodynamics of a single, centrifugal consciousness projecting its thoughts, emotions, and desires onto characters, actions, and locale.[34]

To support his claim Savran uses *The Glass Menagerie*, pointing out that even "a self-proclaimed 'memory play'" such as this one "does not center on Tom."[35]

Yet Savran does not see Williams' early works as realistic any more than Corrigan does. The difference, however, is that Savran believes Williams' plays are "most properly labeled . . . surrealist" rather than expressionist,[36] which, for Savran, is a crucial distinction. His basis for seeing the early plays as surrealistic rests on his claim that they "abound in incidents and scenic elements that shatter the conventions of domestic realism and challenge the notion of the spectacle as empirical replica."[37] He sees Williams' call in the production notes to *The Glass Menagerie* for a "new plastic theatre," one that will "take the place of the exhausted theatre of realistic conventions," as a *surrealist* desire.[38] Savran uses the example of *Camino Real* to support his claim that Williams' early plays are surrealistic. But since *Camino Real* (1953) was a self-conscious departure on Williams' part from the forms of his earlier dramas, and indeed an exception in terms of form to all his drama up to and including *The Night of the Iguana*,[39] it is not a representative example of Williams' early plays.

While Savran has a point insofar that Williams' early plays do not correspond to "the expressionist model," substituting the nonrealistic term "surrealist" for the nonrealistic term "expressionist" is not very helpful. The features of surrealism that propose to distort external reality, such as the use of dreamlike images and an alternative ordering of reality which defies logic, space, and time, are found in many plays considered to be expressionistic as well. In fact, both expressionism and surrealism laid the roots for what Martin Esslin termed the "Theatre of the Absurd," where the form and technique of both these movements merge to the point at which they become virtually indistinguishable. Savran is correct in saying that no early Williams play "stages the psychodynamics of a single, centrifugal consciousness," but neither does any early play (with the clear exception of *Camino Real*) entirely "shatter the conventions of domestic realism." Williams' early plays, while certainly employing nonrealistic devices, remain essentially realistic in terms of action, character, and language, especially when compared with overtly antirealistic dramas, such as *Camino Real* or the work of such so-called absurdist dramatists as Samuel Beckett or Eugène Ionesco. His symbolic devices are not incompatible with the essentially realistic form his early drama embraces. *Menagerie* is realistic in its use of language as a representation of essential truths and, aside from some unrealistic conventions, in its fourth-wall illusionism. The fact that Williams, in *The Glass Menagerie*, may be seen as "def[ying] logic, space, and time" insofar that *Menagerie* is a "memory play" does not take away from the fact that within the action of the play itself logic, space, and time remain consistent and correspond to the central illusion of dramatic realism: the illusion that stage presentation is able to objectively represent an unmediated reality.

Savran is also correct in pointing out that Williams himself saw *The Glass Menagerie* as part of "a conception of a new, plastic theatre which must take the place of the exhausted theatre of realistic conventions if the theatre is to resume vitality as a part of our culture" (production notes to *Menagerie*, 1:131). Williams saw conventional realism, a mode of representation which purportedly strove for freedom from "artificial" dramatic conventions, as precisely depending on its own burdensome, superficial conventions, which prevented the artist access to the truth. He felt that the artist had a responsibility to deal closely with reality and "truth," but that the flat, limited realism of rigid conventions was not the best way to try and grasp the deeper meanings of living in the world. Therefore, Williams' brand of realism made use of certain nondiegetic devices such as "a free, imaginative use of light" (*Menagerie*, 1:134) and music which is given symbolic significance, devices often associated with symbolism, expressionism, or surrealism, in an effort to move beyond external appearances. Williams' realism is highly symbolic, and therefore a play such as *The Glass Menagerie* is not strictly realistic in formal terms. Perhaps this is what led Williams to the conclusion that "the opening night audience had never seen this kind of theater before."[40] From the beginning of his career Williams asserted that his work was "an innovation in theatre," that he was doing something new.[41] However, he was still depending heavily on the conventions of realism in terms of dramatic action, plot, character construction, and the signifying powers of language as a direct expression of the real, as opposed to employing a more non-realistic dramaturgy which would, for example, rely less on action and plot, present characters as representatives of abstractions (such as emotions or points of view) rather than as complex psychological subjects, and embrace a minimalistic language which deliberately calls attention to its own indeterminacy.

Critics have argued for *Menagerie's* antirealism on the basis that Williams originally intended to divert the audience's attention from the illusions of realistic presentation by making use of a screen "on which were projected magic-lantern slides bearing images or titles" (production notes to *Menagerie*, 1:132)—a device reminiscent of Bertolt Brecht's placards and films, which were intended to produce in the audience a sense of critical detachment from the drama, an alienation effect as opposed to realistic identification. Williams' screen device, however, was omitted from the acting version of the play by its producer, Eddie Dowling, both in the first production at the Civic Theatre in Chicago and in the original Broadway production. It is important to note that Williams did not flatly object to this omission as a radical distortion of his supposedly antirealistic intentions for the play. In the production notes to *Menagerie* he writes that he did not regret this omission, since the performance of Laurette Taylor, the original Amanda Wingfield, was "powerful" enough to sustain the play, making it "suitable to have the utmost simplicity in the physical production" (1:132).

It seems that Williams' original intentions for the screen images was to "give accent to certain values in each scene" (production notes to *Menagerie*, 1:132), an emphasis which he later felt was unnecessary given the powerful performance of Laurette Taylor. He apparently saw the screen images as a device which unnecessarily *complicated* the production, in contrast to the "simplicity" he felt was more "suitable." But the fact that the screen images and titles were intended as a nondiegetic device which Williams felt would help emphasize the "values" of the play (1:132) indicates his ambivalence concerning realistic presentation as it was currently typical. While Williams desired to represent intangible truths in *Menagerie,* he felt that the limited discursive language of realism needed to be supplemented in order to arrive at these truths more effectively, and in fact the published version of the play retains the screen devices. *However,* he (on the advice of Dowling) reverts back to a dependence on realistic dialogue and performance in the production of the play, as it was the "extraordinary power of Miss Taylor's performance" (1:132), her presentation of the character Amanda through Williams' language, which made the screen images unnecessary. The original purpose of the screen images was not to emphasize that *Menagerie* is an antirealistic work, but in fact to emphasize unambiguously the realistic desire to represent accurately truths or values in the play. Unlike the case of Brecht's epic theater, where the screen images were designed to resist identification and sympathy, Williams' screen images were intended to *strengthen* the audience's identification with the characters and their views as presented on stage.

Another main reason for critics seeing *Menagerie* as antirealistic is a device of central importance to the drama, that of Tom as narrator, which would seem to be incompatible with realism. Tom himself, in his first monologue, makes a point of stating that the play is not realistic, but "sentimental," indicating that it rests on romantic subjectivity (selective "memory") and excessive emotion, rather than the illusion of objectivity which is central to realism. Yet *Menagerie* remains essentially realistic in its representation of a situation which is recognizable to audiences in terms of the established codes which society uses to define external reality. *Menagerie* does not attempt to represent *directly* the fragmented logic of a subjective internal psychology on the stage, as an antirealistic drama typically would. Rather than seeking to undermine the realistic form of the play, Tom's monologues serve to *translate* the subjectivity ("memory") of the "author" (Tom Wingfield, in this case) into an objective social situation represented on the stage primarily through action, mise-en-scène, and language. The play is, after all, a composition in Tom's mind. In effect, the experience of Tom in the *past* is represented through the overall dramaturgy typical of any performance. On the other hand, it is true that Tom's particular *subjective relationship in the present* to the "memory" that is represented in the main action of the play is dramatized as well, but it is represented essentially through discursive language, the language of his monologues, rather than through the action and the mise-en-scène. Tom is therefore constructed and identified with in two ways: the Tom of the past seeks identification as a character in the main action of the play, and the Tom of the present—the narrator—seeks identification through the narrative speeches that serve, in part, to dramatize the existence of this Tom "in the now," who is meant to be perceived and identified with in much the same way that any character of realism is. Therefore, both the character Tom of the "past" and the narrator Tom of the "present" ultimately fulfil a realistic purpose.

Unlike, for example, the narrative device of the Stage Manager in Thornton Wilder's *Our Town* (1938), Tom's commentary as an observer actually seeks to *enhance* rather than resist the illusion of reality by its communication of "truth" through language, as its objective is the transformation (the explanation) of a scene or situation in Tom's mind into linguistic/dramatic representation. Tom's appearance as narrator/commentator interrupts the realistic fourth-wall illusion only before, after, and between scenes. In the action of the drama itself he is a character conforming to the illusions of realism. Wilder's Stage Manager, on the other hand, is very present (both in his moments as commentator and within the "play" itself) as a device that controls the actors and the action on stage—he is, after all, the "stage manager." The boundaries between the Stage Manager's commentary and the internal drama are not as clearly defined as Tom's boundaries in *Menagerie*. The Stage Manager interacts regularly with the characters, clapping his hands as a signal for a particular scene to end,[42] or acknowledging the actors by "tip[ping] his hat to the ladies" (20) and thanking them for their performances (21). At times, he plays minor characters in the internal drama when needed, such as "Mrs. Forrest" (27) or "the clergyman" (77), and steps into the drama to interrupt the action when he feels that the "point" has been made: "Thank you. Thank you! That'll do. We'll have to interrupt again here" (31). Williams, on the other hand, wants the main action of the scenes of the past to retain their realistic illusion—*but* not in complete independence of the Tom of the present. So while he keeps Tom's "roles" of narrator and character separate in one sense, his "drama" includes both Tom's monologues and the realistically presented scenes of the past. In both cases, however, it is essentially realistic effects and the kinds of responses they evoke that Williams is after, unlike Wilder who uses his stage manner more in a Brechtean way.

In *Our Town*, there is a (nonrealistic) consciousness of performance as the Stage Manager introduces the scenes that will follow his commentary, asking the actors for enlightening answers to questions of "universal" importance. In *Menagerie*, however, the main gist of Tom's monologues does not aim for such an all-encompassing scope of vision. Tom's speeches serve to elaborate on the atmosphere of the particular scenes and to supply details which will aid in understanding (from his point of view, of course) the situation and the characters' motivations for their actions, factors which are important to realistic presentation. Compare these two sample narratives:

> *Stage Manager.* Thank you very much, Mr. and Mrs. Webb.—Now I have to interrupt again here. You see, we want to know how all this began—the wedding, this plan to spend a lifetime together. I'm awfully interested in how big things like that begin.
> You know how it is: you're twenty-one or twenty-two and you make some decisions; then whisssh! you're seventy: you've been a lawyer for fifty years, and that white-haired lady at your side has eaten over fifty thousand meals with you.
> How do such things begin?
>
> (*Our Town*, 60)

> *Tom.* After the fiasco at Rubicam's Business College, the idea of getting a gentleman caller for Laura began to play a more and more important part in Mother's calculations. It became an obsession. Like some archetype of the universal unconscious, the image of the gentleman caller haunted our small apartment.
>
> (1:159)

The characters in *Our Town* are not characters in the same sense as Williams' characters—they are symbols that serve to represent what Wilder sees as the universal aspects of living and growing up; they are performing for the audience a dramatization of how "such things [as love and marriage] begin," and the Stage Manager's use of the collective "you" emphasizes the common aspect of experience that is being represented. Wilder writes in the preface to *Three Plays* that

> It is through the theatre's power to raise the exhibited individual action into the realm of idea and type and universal that it is able to evoke our belief. . . . *Our Town* is not offered as a picture of life in a New Hampshire village; or as a speculation of life after death. . . . It is an attempt to find a value above all price for the smallest events in our daily life. I have made the claim as preposterous as possible, for I have set the village against the largest dimensions of time and place.[43]

Our Town is not realistically presented, and the Stage Manager is a blatantly antirealistic element of the play—an alienating device—

which is a main part of its conception. He serves to interrupt any realistic illusion that the audience might be drawn into (as he literally interrupts the action at several points) and focus its attention towards the universal issues that the drama self-consciously explores.

The situation and characters Williams presents in *Menagerie,* on the other hand, are much more *specific,* much more realistic, as *Menagerie* strives for a recreation of everyday life and a representation of "real" human beings. Williams does not conceive of "character" in *Menagerie* as simply symbolic "role." The characters in the play are meant to represent actual human beings in all their complexity, a goal which works within the illusions of realism. Moreover, the language of Tom's speeches, rather than interrupting the action and *alienating* the audience, actually seeks the audience's *identification* with Tom, aligning the members of the audience with his perspective and giving them access to his thoughts (with all their poetic nuances) so that we may understand him better. Therefore, in this sense as well as in the translation of internal perception into language and objective social situation, Tom's narration deliberately serves the goals of realism rather than undermining them.

The fact that Tom retains his identity both as narrator and as a character in the internal drama is yet another factor which aids in furthering the goals of realism, since Tom Wingfield is seen as a "real person" (in his role as narrator) who is relating the story of a crucial experience, a defining moment in his "life" which had affected the choices he went on to make. Tom could even be seen as fulfilling the function of the narrator of realistic fiction with regard to Laura and Amanda. Like David Copperfield, who begins Dickens' novel by wondering whether he will be "the hero of [his] own life" as he sets out to narrate the story, Tom is the same "person" as narrator that he is as character. Therefore, not only is this story itself told realistically, but even the "nonrealistic" narrative device can be seen as participating in the illusion that the characters are particular individuals rather than the symbolic representatives of certain types, as they are in *Our Town* or, in a different manner, in *Camino Real.* In the foreword to *Camino Real* Williams writes that "its people are mostly archetypes of certain basic attitudes and qualities with those mutations that would occur if they had continued along the road to this hypothetical terminal point in it." "A convention of the play," he adds, "is existence outside of time in a place of no specific locality. If you regard it that way, I suppose it becomes an elaborate allegory"

(2:419). The characters in *Camino Real* are taken from history, mythology, legend, and previous literature. Williams removes them from their established historical or literary contexts and brings them together in a newly constructed one—a practice common to antirealistic presentation.[44] The characters in *The Glass Menagerie*, on the other hand, are named in such a way as to suggest that they are specific individuals in the contemporary social environment.

Although most of Williams' early plays could be said to end with some type of realistic closure, some may argue that *Menagerie* is an exception, that no determined sense of an ending exists at the end of *Menagerie*, and that the play is simply obliterated as Tom directs Laura to "blow out [her] candles" (1:237). Yet obliteration can certainly be seen as closure, and we do get a sense that a story has been told. *Menagerie* clearly provides closure for Tom and, arguably, for Laura and Amanda as well. The departure of "the gentleman caller," who represented their last chance for survival in a society which has rejected them, has left Amanda and especially Laura with no viable alternative. Amanda's closing speech to Tom makes it evident that their world is over:

> Don't think about us, a mother deserted, an unmarried sister who's crippled and has no job! Don't let anything interfere with your selfish pleasure! Just go, go, go—to the movies. . . . Go, then! Go to the moon—you selfish dreamer! (1:236)

Tom's final speech indicates closure for at least his role in the play:

> I didn't go to the moon, I went much further—for time is the longest distance between two places. . . . I left St. Louis. I descended the steps of this fire escape for the last time and followed, from then on, in my father's footsteps, attempting to find in motion what was lost in space. (1:236–37)

Tom's closing monologue can even be said to resemble the close of a realistic novel, as *it provides closure from Tom's—the narrator's— point of view,* and therefore exhibits the emphasis on individual experience and individual perspective that the realistic novel embraces while focusing on the fully-formed self that resulted from his experience:

> Oh, Laura, Laura, I tried to leave you behind me, but I am more faithful than I intended to be! I reach for a cigarette, I cross the street,

I run into the movies or a bar . . .   anything that can blow your candles out! (1:237)

The omission of and debate over the nondiegetic devices in the original script of *The Glass Menagerie* may have led Williams to a much more subtle use of them in his next play, *A Streetcar Named Desire*. As in *Menagerie*, Williams uses music and lighting symbolically in *Streetcar*, but the more overt nonrealistic devices, such as images and titles projected on a screen or a narrator who comments on the action of the drama are missing. All the nonrealistic moments in *Streetcar* can be accounted for by the fact that they take place in Blanche's mind. They therefore contribute to a realistic purpose by attempting to represent what is going on in her "thoughts" so as to allow the audience access to the information it needs to identify with her and *understand* her character. For instance, the "polka music" which is present in Blanche's mind as she tells the story of the night her young husband shot himself is represented aloud onstage and is in that sense nonrealistic (1:355). However, Williams' introduction of music in this context ultimately serves a realistic purpose since it emphasizes the distinction between fantasy and reality in the world of the play. Moreover, it exists to further develop the illusion that Blanche is an actual human being with possession of a "mind" that is on the verge of instability. The most prominent antirealistic moment comes during the last scene, when Blanche has gone mad and is being taken away to the asylum. But the "Lurid reflections [that] appear on the walls in odd, sinuous shapes," the distorted music of the Varsouviana, and the echoes that rise and fall are all *deliberate representations of the unreal*—of Blanche's madness (1:414–16). In *Streetcar*, there is a clear-cut distinction between Blanche's fantasy world and the realm of reality in which the characters interact.

Williams' next major work after *Streetcar*, *Cat on a Hot Tin Roof*, was virtually free of the kinds of nondiegetic devices that were present in his earlier plays, and so it was more difficult for critics to see this play as a "protest against realism."[45] Yet there has been critical disagreement concerning whether the poetic speeches of Williams' early work fall under the heading of realistic dialogue, and during the New York rehearsal period of *Cat on a Hot Tin Roof*, Williams and the director, Elia Kazan, debated over the presentation of these speeches. Kazan proposed that Burl Ives in the part of Big Daddy should walk "down to the edge of the forestage before the beginning of that long uninterrupted speech [Williams had] given him, . . . look the audience right in the eye, and speak it directly to them. Straight out, as if it were a concert."[46] He writes that he and set designer Jo Mielziner "had read the play in the same way":

> [W]e saw its great merit was its brilliant rhetoric and its theatricality. Jo didn't see the play as realistic any more than I did. If it was to be done realistically, I would have to contrive stage business to keep the old man talking those great second-act speeches turned out front and pretend that it was just another day in the life of the Pollitt family. . . . It didn't seem like just another day in the life of a cotton planter's family to Jo or to me; it seemed like the best kind of theatre, the kind we were interested in encouraging, the theatre theatrical, not pretending any longer that an audience wasn't out there to be addressed but having a performer as great as Burl Ives acknowledge their presence at all times and even make eye contact with individuals.[47]

Williams objected to this acknowledgement of the audience on the grounds that *Cat* was "a realistic play." While Kazan doubted "that in the Mississippi delta country, old cotton planters talk that eloquently and that long without interruption," Williams insisted that yes, they did, since "Who'd dare interrupt him?"[48] The central point is that Williams' poetic language, rather than emphasizing the antirealism of his plays, is used to construct and develop the characters who use it. Characters who express themselves in "poetic" language in Williams' plays are not meant to be seen as "unrealistic," but rather as realistic characters who speak in a poetic manner. In realistic drama, the type of language a character employs gives the audience a sense of who the character "is."

Treatment of the setting was another area where Kazan and Williams disagreed. Williams insisted that *Cat* was to be done realistically, but Kazan and Jo Mielziner didn't agree:

> I caused Jo to design our setting as I wished, a large, triangular platform, tipped toward the audience and holding only one piece of furniture, an ornate bed. This brought the play down to its essentials and made it impossible for it to be played except as I preferred.[49]

Kazan's resistance to seeing *Cat* as realistic rested on his view of the play as "theatrical," as art which is deliberately conscious of its own performance. The "glorious" language of *Cat* was one aspect of this (antirealistic) theatricality for Kazan, yet Williams disagreed with his reading. Once when discussing realistic dialogue with Dotson Rader, Williams advised him: "Baby, don't write how people talk. Write how we *think* they talk. It is what we think we hear, not what they actually say, that sounds true."[50]

The fact that Williams' speeches were often seen as "poetic" did not make them any less realistic for Williams in the context of the action. Like *The Glass Menagerie* and *A Streetcar Named Desire*, *Cat on a Hot Tin Roof* is a realistic play whose overall dramaturgy aims for a representation of truth through the referential codes of external reality, despite the unrealistic touches Kazan and Mielziner may have given the play in performance. Mielziner's minimalistic set design and his focus on the "ornate bed" as the center of the action does not take away from *Cat*'s essentially realistic core. Moreover, as stage conventions shift away from complete verisimilitude (André Antoine's Théâtre Libre of the late nineteenth century, for example, insisted on real food, elaborate furnishings, and even real fountains for its productions), modern audiences are not at all "alienated" by minimalistic scenery. In fact, the conception of character, action, and language, along with the avoidance of nondiegetic devices in *Cat on a Hot Tin Roof* makes it, perhaps, Williams' most realistic work.

While it may seem at this point that my argument has been strongly emphasizing the realistic aspects of Williams' early work, the ideological complications and contradictions of realistic presentation were clearly in his mind when he wrote these plays, and I want to be careful not to gloss over that fact. My choice to emphasize the essentially realistic form of the early plays in this chapter serves to establish a distinction between the dramatic style of these works and that of the later plays, which presented language, character, and action in a very different manner, and with very different goals in mind. These differences are crucial in understanding the later reactions of the critical establishment, which repeatedly emphasized how Williams had "changed" during the 1960s. Unlike the experimental later work, Williams' early work only marginally questions the major tenet of realistic drama that language and action are able to represent an intangible truth located somewhere outside language. The problems associated with this notion, however, are evident, and his abundant use of symbolic devices during the early years suggests that Williams was quite aware of these problems. Levine addresses realism's prime objective, reminding us that "The quest for unmediated experience becomes central to the dramatic tensions of most realistic fiction."[51] However, one of the contradictions of realism is, of course, that the signifying codes which constitute reality can in fact only represent themselves; no stability of reference actually exists. Since language is the most accessible of these codes, dramatic realism, like narrative fiction, relies heavily on language's supposed access to an unmediated reality—yet it is impossible for language to reflect any outer reality precisely because it is a closed, independent system:

> As we may by now be tired of hearing, language, in representing reality, most forcefully demonstrates reality's absence. At best, language creates the illusion of reality so that our current definitions of realism swerve from implying the possibility of direct representation to focus on the difference between the medium and the reality whose absence it registers. Language, finally, can "represent" only other language.[52]

Historically, those employing realistic forms in literature desired to reject the "artificial" language and conventions associated with earlier forms such as romanticism or, in the case of drama, the "well-made play." Yet while rejecting previously established conventions, realism inevitably created new ones. Levine describes the struggle and the contradiction of realism's desire to represent, primarily through language, an unmediated truth or reality:

> my focus will be on the struggle inherent in any "realist" effort—the struggle to avoid the inevitable conventionality of language in pursuit of the unattainable unmediated reality. Realism, as a literary method, can in these terms be defined as a self-conscious effort, usually in the name of some moral enterprise of truth telling and extending the limits of human sympathy, to make literature appear to be describing directly not some other language but reality itself (whatever that may be taken to be); in this effort, the writer must self-contradictorily dismiss previous conventions of representation while, in effect, establishing new ones.[53]

It seems that the contradiction between Williams' dissatisfaction with conventional realism and his simultaneous embrace of an essentially realistic mode in his early plays stems from his own struggle and ambivalence concerning the representation of truth. During his early period Williams was unable to dismiss realism with its reliance on referential codes—most especially language— as a direct mode of access to the real, but at some level he sensed the inadequacy of these codes, leading him to experiment with antircalistic forms in plays such as *The Purification* and *Camino Real*.

Politically, realism is a mode of representation which functions ideologically in the realm of industrial capitalism. Belsey writes that

> It is in the epoch of capitalism that ideology emphasizes the value of individual freedom, freedom of conscience and, of course, consumer choice in all the multiplicity of its forms. The ideology of liberal humanism assumes a world of non-contradictory (and therefore fundamentally unalterable) individuals whose unfettered consciousness is the origin of meaning, knowledge, and action. . . . Classic realism, still the dominant mode in literature, film and television drama, roughly coincides chronologically with the epoch of industrial capitalism. It performs, I wish to suggest, the work of ideology, not only in its representation of a world of consistent subjects who are the origin of meaning, knowledge, and action, but also in offering the reader [or viewer], as the position from which the text is most readily intelligible, the position of subject as the origin both of understanding and of action in accordance with that understanding.[54]

The human subject (and its representation in the form of "character") in realistic literature is seen as a unified, unfragmented "individual" subject acting consistently with its desires, which are able to be known and articulated. While Belsey is discussing realism as a mode of representation which is compatible with the ideological goals of industrial capitalism in terms of its construction of both character and audience as sovereign subjects, Williams' realistic plays exhibit an awareness of the ironic link between realism as a literary form which reinforces an industrial capitalist view of the subject as "the origin of meaning, knowledge, and action," and industrial capitalism itself as a force which undermines any sovereignty his characters may experience in society. Williams' early plays clearly perform the work of formal realism in terms of their representation of the human subject, but his themes often deal with the tragic effect that capitalism has on the characters—especially the women—in his plays. His early work therefore remains essentially realistic not only in terms of the mode of representation he chose, but also in terms of the subject of representation—the social order of industrial capitalism and the plight of "the individual left watching the twentieth century sweep by."[55] At the same time, however, his early plays offer a subtle but powerful challenge to realism's ideological goals by manipulating the mythology of industrial capitalism rather than completely reinforcing it. In fact, Williams' *very* early work (pre-1945) includes left-wing WPA propaganda plays which are *specifically* critical of capitalism, but these plays were too blatantly and didactically political to gain him any widespread critical acclaim. Williams' political views were represented in a much more subtle manner with *The Glass Menagerie*, however, and in this play as well as in his subsequent early successes capitalism emerges as the new world order which ultimately devours rather than empowers his characters.

As early as *The Glass Menagerie*, Williams had clearly begun to present his vision of modern society. *Menagerie* is in fact a social play about a family living in a St. Louis tenement,

> one of those vast hive-like conglomerations of cellular living-units that flower as warty growths in overcrowded urban centers of lower middle-class population and are symptomatic of the impulse of this largest and fundamentally enslaved section of American society to avoid fluidity and differentiation and to exist and function as one interfused mass of automatism. (*Menagerie* stage direction, 1:143)

Williams is writing about a life he knew in the modern world that was changing all around him and the rest of the American public. He represents America during the height of the 1930s depression, before the Second World War, as the protagonists of the play, dislocated and frustrated, struggle to find their places in the new society which was increasingly dependent on industry and technology. In "The Failure of Technology in *The Glass Menagerie*," James Reynolds points out that

> Laura's fragile collection of glass animals gives [*The Glass Menagerie*] its name and a central symbol with both an esthetic and a personal focus. But the play is punctuated with another set of references, an array of ordinary products of twentieth-century technology, that expands its significance beyond the personal even as it illuminates the lives of its protagonists.[56]

Menagerie is certainly a very personal play in terms of the conflicts among the characters themselves and their individual searches for some kind of satisfaction beyond the St. Louis slums. Yet the personal merges very strongly with the social in this play, as all the characters are engulfed by the rapidly changing, alienating American capitalist system in which they are expected not only to survive but to find happiness as well. Reynolds comments on the effects of technology on *Menagerie's* characters in a society which was becoming increasingly capitalist:

> One pattern that looms in the background of the Wingfield family is the way that changing economic and social modes can restrict the potential for happy and successful lives. We are always aware of Amanda's grand past in the Old South, her wealthy suitors and her servants, as we watch her make do in a walkup tenement. And Tom and Laura are pushed into commercial careers that conflict with their temperaments and aspirations.[57]

The characters' adjustments to modern urban life are a central part of their personal conflicts. Riddel claims that in *The Glass Menagerie* "Williams gets in his social licks while groping for a more universal statement."[58] In her essay "The Synthetic Myth," Esther Merle Jackson writes that in *Menagerie*

> Williams began to create myths of modern life; that is, he began to weave the dark images of his personal vision together with certain sociological, psychological, religious, and philosophical contents, in a schematic explication of modern life.[59]

None of the characters in *Menagerie* are immune to the alienating powers of industrial capitalism. Grigor Pavlov, in a 1968 article for *Annuaire de l'Université de Sofia,* has compared Jim—the gentleman caller who enters the realm of the Wingfield family with dreams of "Knowledge—Zzzzzp! Money—Zzzzzp!—Power!" (1:222) which he plans to achieve through industry—to Arthur Miller's Willie Loman. Even Jim, the "potential entrepreneur of technological capitalism,"[60] is only

> another member of the blind American middle-class [who] just doesn't realize that men's destinies under capitalism are not shaped by personal virtues and self-perfection but by the operation of the ruthless economic laws of capitalistic development.[61]

The Glass Menagerie is a play which deals with the social realities of a changing world, a world in which the protagonists are supposed to function as subjects in control of their lives, but are in fact subjected to the overwhelming powers of capitalism. The fact that Laura blows out her candles at the end of the play signifies not only *her* obliteration, but the obliteration of all the characters in some sense. Displaced and dislocated from the social realm, the protagonists all "disappear."

The struggle to maintain control in a world which is changing rapidly is also evident *A Streetcar Named Desire*. In this play, one of Williams' most naturalistic, the dramatic tension rests in the battle between Blanche, a faded belle of the old South whose principles will no longer assure her survival in an increasingly pragmatic urbanized world, and Stanley, a deliberately sexual, "down-to-earth" laborer with a certain "animal joy" (1:264) who represents what has been characterized as "reality" by Williams and by the critical establishment in general. Riddel speaks of "Stanley's realistic self,"[62] and Alvin B. Kernan writes that "We are presented in *Streetcar* with two polar ways of looking at experience: the realistic view of Stanley Kowalski and the 'nonrealistic' view of his sister-in-law, Blanche DuBois."[63] In this context the term *realistic* refers both to a perception of the world which realism endorses—one that opposes an idealized or romanticized interpretation of experience—and also to the form in which the drama is presented. Blanche's nostalgia for the past and her idealization of human behavior can therefore be described as a "nonrealistic view" of the world, although it is a view which is certainly represented realistically. Survival of the fittest is the issue here, and it is clear that what characterizes "the fittest" is the ability to "adapt to circumstances," an ability which Blanche ultimately does not possess despite her claims that she does (1:300).

Williams' realistic/naturalistic representation of the world has often been challenged and criticized as sentimental, apolitical, and fatally deterministic. In a 1948 article for the journal *Masses and Mainstream*, one of the first critical articles to appear on Williams' work, Harry Taylor chides Williams for what he sees as the lack of dramatic conflict and social significance in his plays. He claims that Williams' philosophy has not yet been developed, and that

> Williams, as a direct consequence of his socio-philosophical position, has been unable to achieve conflict. Confrontations, yes, and savage, almost animal. . . . Great drama cannot emerge out of flight and hysteria, but arises from genuine conflict, an element that can only be generated by the writer's conviction that the battle is vital and that the means to wage it exist.[64]

Referring to *Streetcar*, Taylor claims that Williams is "the prisoner of a view in which the dominant reality is monstrously destructive and implacable," and that he has "once more [in *Streetcar*] opposed [this reality] with a poor, hazy-minded being already broken in the toils and armed only with obstinate illusions rather than with reasonable will."[65] What Taylor seems to be objecting to is the naturalistic philosophy Williams represents in his early plays, most notably *Menagerie* and *Streetcar*. Taylor's advice to Williams is that he

> will write greatly only if he can re-examine reality and emotionally recognize what his intellect may already have grasped: that the forces of good in this world are adult and possess both the will and the power to change our environment. He needs but the merest extraversion, the briefest glance at human history to see these forces in operation.[66]

While this objection to a philosophy which represents destinies as fixed and individual alterity/alterability as only an illusion comes as no surprise from a journal called *Masses and Mainstream*, Taylor's attack on Williams is unjustified. In 1977 George Niesen wrote that the result of Williams' realistic world view in his plays is one of "standard dramatic conflict with strong social content."[67] The kind of "dramatic conflict" which Taylor suggests—a battle between good and evil in which "the forces of good" come out the victor—is reductionistic and uncomplicated. As characters, Stanley and Blanche are certainly not simple representations of good and evil. In fact, if one were to try and impose these labels upon the characters it would be difficult to know which label to assign to which protagonist.

Taylor writes that "great drama cannot be evoked from the opposition of will with non-will but only by the firmly engaged conflict of powerful wills."[68] It is not that the wills of Blanche and Stanley are of unequal strength, as Taylor suggests—that Blanche is simply "poor" and "hazy-minded" while Stanley represents a reality which is "monstrously destructive and implacable." There is certainly no lack of dramatic conflict in *Streetcar*. Only an imperceptive reader could align Blanche with "non-will," as she puts up a notable fight for survival. First, she tries to hold on to the Southern aristocratic life she knows, telling Stella that she "stayed and fought for [Belle Reve], bled for it, almost died for it!" (1:260). Once Belle Reve is "lost," however, she arrives at the home of her sister and attempts to influence Stanley first through flirtation, flaunting her feminine "charm" and jasmine perfume, and then by claiming to "[lay her] cards on the table" (1:281). When that attempt fails, Blanche tells Stella to "face the facts" that she's "married to a madman" (1:313) and pleads with her to leave

Stanley in order to start a new life with her sister. But Stella is perfectly content with her situation, and Blanche's final course of action is to adjust to the new world order to the best of her ability. Her courtship with Mitch is an attempt to use what is still marketable in the modern world—what remains of her "physical beauty" (1:396)—in order to survive.

Blanche's last attempt at emotional and mental survival comes at the end of scene ten, where the confrontation between her and Stanley is like that of two jungle animals, naturalism in its most literal representation in the play. Blanche fights for her sanity as she "smashes a bottle on the table and faces [Stanley], clutching the broken top," threatening to "twist the broken end in [his] face" (1:402). Her final defeat rests in the fact that Blanche and Stanley represent two different world orders, and while there is certainly a strong implication in the play that Blanche's world may in fact be the superior one in terms of the human spirit, Stanley's world happens to be the dominant one, while hers is rapidly declining. Even though Stanley could no more survive in Blanche's world than she can in his, the issue is irrelevant in terms of survival in the context of the play. Stanley's world is the reality of twentieth-century postwar industrial capitalism, and so it is this world order which overtakes Blanche. Williams has called Blanche "a sacrificial victim . . . of society," explaining that she "was not adaptable to the circumstances as they were, that the world had imposed on her."[69]

Taylor ends his article by insisting that it

is no special plea for social plays. But surely the absence of the socio-historic periphery in the author's mind weakens his attack even on personal drama, depriving it of the aura of larger reality and of moral conviction.[70]

There is no "absence of socio-historic periphery" in Williams' mind. While it is true that Blanche loses her struggle because she "never was hard or self-sufficient enough" (1:332), one issue that has often been ignored in discussions of Blanche's delicate constitution and her inability or unwillingness to adjust to "reality" is the fact that she comes to Stanley and Stella because she has no money. Ultimately, it is her financial dependence on Stanley and his decision to send her on a bus "Back to Laurel" (1:376) which defeats her. Like Amanda Wingfield's, Blanche's aristocratic background is useless in the rapidly changing capitalist system restructuring the landscape of American society during the years just before the Second World War and beyond. Belle Reve had been taken by creditors and, fired from her job as a high-school teacher after her search for intimacy had led her to an affair with a seventeen-year-old student, Blanche is left with no independent wealth and no marketable skill. Her one attempt to enter the world of capitalism rests on her hopes that Shep Huntleigh (a real or imaginary college "beau" who is now married) will set her and Stella up in "a shop of some kind" (1:317). But her plans are vague, and Blanche is not exactly an entrepreneur: "Y'know how indifferent I am to money. I think of money in terms of what it does for you" (1:316). While she needs money and sees it as "the way out" (1:315) of her situation, her idea of an "investment" is taking a trip to Miami "thinking [she'd] meet someone with a million dollars" (1:316). Blanche is not self-sufficient enough in a capitalistic society to be able to survive. Moreover, a Southern aristocratic *woman* must depend "on the kindness of strangers," male strangers, for security. Stella found Stanley, and is content to live on his terms. While he is the "stranger" who could have presumably saved Blanche as well, she fights against the world he stands for and so is defeated, along with her "romantic" view of the world. Realism, as both dramatic form and the perception which it endorses, perseveres.

Perhaps the easiest access to the ideology of realism during the 1940s and 1950s was, not unlike today, through the latest Hollywood film production, a medium which enthusiastically embraced the work of Tennessee Williams during his early years. Even in film, however, Williams manages to undermine realism's political goals by illustrating postwar America's problematic relationship with capitalism. Like many of the characters in his early plays, Williams' screenplay protagonists "Baby Doll" and Archie Lee find themselves socially marginalized by the capitalist system and must fight for practical survival after they are swept aside. In the 1956 film *Baby Doll*, directed by Elia Kazan, the old agrarian economic structures which had formerly kept cotton gin owner Archie Lee Meigham in business are fading, as the new social order of industrial capitalism rapidly moves into the South. Represented by the Sicilian from Texas—Silva Vacarro—capitalism comes to Mississippi offering bigger, faster, and cheaper cotton production equipment, and as the film opens this "foreigner" has managed to drive all the local cotton producers, including Archie, out of business. Silva Vacarro's significance as the harbinger of a world in which a man's worth is tied up with his success in business is echoed by his name, which Archie repeatedly points out is "like a silver lining . . . gold or even nickel plated."[71] In a desperate act to reclaim his financial and social position, Archie sets fire to Vacarro's business, hoping that the law will honor the racial and social ties of the traditional community and not investigate too seriously.

With these social issues in the background, the film centers on the marriage between forty-year-old Archie and his young bride, known only as "Baby Doll," emphasizing her childlike dependence and purely decorative function. Baby Doll, who "never got past the fourth grade," was married off to Archie at age eighteen, when her wealthy aristocratic father was dying and wanted his daughter to be able to survive comfortably after he was gone. The virgin bride, however, didn't feel that she was "ready" for marriage, so she and Archie negotiated an "agreement" that while they would live together immediately after the wedding, they would consummate their marriage on her twentieth birthday, and not before. The film's action takes place on the day before this promised occasion, but Baby Doll is not looking forward to her twentieth birthday. While Archie was a successful businessman on the day he married her, his financial situation has since become desperate, and therefore he has not been able to fulfill his end of their "agreement." His house, which was once "the grandest in the Delta," is in total disrepair, they can't afford to have their garbage picked up regularly, and all the furniture—except for the kitchen set and the crib and dressers in the nursery where Baby Doll sleeps alone—has been repossessed.

Virginity is constructed as a commodity in this film, and it is Baby Doll's unrealized sexual potential which defines her. Without a "useful" sexual identity, she is only a "doll"—a piece of plastic—not a fully realized human being. Throughout the film Baby Doll's attempts at gaining financial independence from Archie are thwarted by her lack of practical skills, and she constantly resorts to flirting and teasing in order to try and manipulate her situation. She keeps threatening to "move to the Kotton King hotel," even tries to register by using her maiden name and appealing to her late father's status in the community, but the only way she can escape her situation in the new economic system is through the possession of capital. She therefore contemplates getting a job—suggesting to Archie that she could "be a cashier" among other things, but his response is mocking as he reminds her that she "can't count change." On her one trip into town accompanying Archie to the doctor, she tries to get a job as a receptionist in the adjacent dentist's office, flirting with the den-list to compensate for the fact that she can't type. He participates in the flirtation briefly, but she is finally told that she "has to know typing" or they "can't use her."

Like Blanche and Amanda, Baby Doll has no marketable skill and no independent wealth, but she manages to maintain some kind of power and control over her life by carefully guarding and using the only commodity she has—her sexual promise. When Vacarro asks her if she intends to honor her agreement with Archie on her twentieth birthday, she replies that it "depends . . . on whether or not the furniture comes back." After strongly suspecting that Archie was responsible for burning down his cotton factory, Vacarro offers him his remaining business in the hopes of gaining access to Archie's factory and finding evidence of the arson. He sends Archie across the river to get a new piece of equipment, and—at Archie's insistence that Baby Doll "entertain" their guest—spends the afternoon with Baby Doll attempting to get a confession via seduction from the young woman. She finally does sign a confession, but in the meantime a genuine attraction develops between them. When Archie returns, he suspects that Vacarro has seduced his wife, and even though their association never went beyond a kiss, they unite in an attempt to humiliate Archie and blackmail him into giving Vacarro control of the business. Baby Doll therefore attempts to gain power by breaking her "agreement" with Archie and aligning herself with Vacarro, the visible representative of the new promise which industrial capitalism offers. She uses her sexuality as a bargaining tool in order to get the best deal.

The other woman in this film—Baby Doll's spinster aunt Rose, the sister of her father—is past her prime as a sexual commodity, but has managed to survive by drifting from one relative's house to another, making herself useful by cooking the family meals. She lives currently with Archie and Baby Doll, but Archie is dissatisfied with her services and finally tells her that she must leave. It is Vacarro—the new savior—who offers Aunt Rose a "deal" and asks her to come live with him as his cook. Vacarro has replaced Archie as the new, more potent protector and keeper of the social order. In reply to Baby Doll's frustration that "Sometimes I don't know where to go or what to do!" Vacarro announces the dictum of a changing world order:

People come into this world without instructions of where to go or what to do, so they wander a little and then go away—drift for a while and then vanish. And so make room for newcomers. Going and coming back and forth—rush, rush. Permanence? Nothing.

The old world in which Archie had power through "position," "friends," and "long standing business associates" in the community is usurped by the *new* force in town—the "Wop" whose power is guaranteed through his ability to negotiate and produce. Yet although it is clear at the end of the film that capitalism as a system will win out, Archie still tries desperately to regain power: first, physically, by furiously attempting to kill Vacarro and, that failing, through subsequent negotiations. He appeals to the sheriff as "one white man to another" and "a married man" himself who would understand that Archie Lee's property has been "violated" in more ways than one. He looks to the old values for support, and it is finally this revelation that Vacarro might have invaded Archie's property rights by sleeping with his wife that inspires the law to question the validity of Vacarro's claim that Archie burnt down his cotton gin and then tried to kill him. They arrest Archie only "for appearance sake," and the outcome of "tomorrow" is left ambiguous, since Vacarro *does* have the signed confession of Baby Doll as "an affidavit" to insure that the destruction of his property will not go unpunished. The systematic impersonality of written legal documents is pitted against the tradition of an informal justice system based on a man's word, his background, and his personal ties in the community—and the future is left uncertain. In this transition of power, it is, of course, the women who are forgotten and most dependent on its whims. The film's final segment shows Baby Doll and Aunt Rose standing on the front porch after Archie Lee has been taken away and Vacarro has left to take care of his ultimate priority—"business"—with a promise to return tomorrow. With no power to alter their situation, Baby Doll surrenders herself to the anticipated kindness of the foreign stranger as she sighs to Aunt Rose in the last speech of the film: "Well, let's go in now. We got nothing to do but wait for tomorrow, and see if we're remembered or forgotten." While the triumph of an industrial capitalist world view is left more ambiguous here than in *Streetcar*, the impersonal and disempowering nature of capitalism that Williams portrays clearly denounces the mythology of realism in this realistic narrative of the American South, illustrating once again Williams' uneasy relationship with the dominant mode of representation he chose for his early works. As he became able to articulate more fully this uneasiness with realism that was evident during the first half of his career in his marginal symbolic devices and ideological rebellion, he began to move toward dramatic forms which had more room to explore and embrace the inconsistencies and fragmentation of the real.

3

The Fusion of Pun and Poetry: A Movement toward "Freer Forms"

"Sometimes the truth is more accessible when you ignore realism, because when you see things in a somewhat exaggerated form you capture more of the true essence of life."
—Tennessee Williams, interview with Cecil Brown, 1974

"Mark hasn't shown any marked preference for figurative or conventional styles of. He's gone through drip, fling, sopped, stained, saturated, scraped, ripped, cut, skeins of, mounds of heroically enduring color, but now he's arrived at a departure that's a real departure that I doubt he'll return from."
—Miriam, *In the Bar of a Tokyo Hotel* (7:41)

THROUGHOUT THE 1960S WILLIAMS WAS BECOMING INCREASINGLY suspicious of realism's desire to naturalize the relationship between stage presentation and outside world. He began to question seriously its claim that codes such as referential language could completely articulate thoughts and ideas in an effort to faithfully present human experience, and instead began to discover dramatic forms which examined the signifier's power to *create* rather than represent reality. In several interviews throughout the 1960s Williams amply indicated a desire to write plays that differed from his earlier work, but his descriptions of exactly what he wanted to do differently are often vague and imprecise. In a 1962 interview, he told Lewis Funke and John E. Booth:

> I've been writing too much on the nose, you know, and I've always sensed the fact that life was too ambiguous to be . . . to be presented in a cut and dried fashion. I've always been conscious of that, but I think I'm getting surer now.[1]

In the same interview Williams expressed a desire to move away from the "long speeches" of his early work toward a more minimalistic "gun-fire dialogue" (quoted in chapter one), a desire clearly indicative of a new direction in dramatic writing which was to dominate the work of his later period. Rather than continue to invest in the slice-of-life illusions of his earlier dramas, he wanted to experiment with a dramaturgy which challenged and explored the representational abilities of both language and the non-verbal codes which signify reality. By the early 1970s, Williams was able to articulate more fully the changes that he was making in his dramaturgy. In a 1972 interview with Jim Gaines, Williams explained what he felt were the differences between his earlier and his later work:

> I've certainly grown less naturalistic, in the Sixties very much less. I think that I'm growing into a more direct form, one that fits people and societies going a bit mad, you know? I believe that a new form, if I continue to work in the theater, will come out of it. I shall certainly never work in a long play form for Broadway again. I want to do something quite different. I'm very interested in the presentational form of theater, where everything is very free and different, where you have total license.[2]

Williams' interest in "free and different" dramatic forms had been present during his early period, in plays such as *The Purification* (1945; pub. 1953), a one-act piece which, as I pointed out in chapter one, Williams described in the published text as "a play in verse to be performed with musical accompaniment on the guitar" (6:40) and, of course, in the full-length play *Camino Real*, which, in the introduction to the play, he calls an "elaborate allegory" (2:419) with an intense degree of "freedom and mobility of form" (2:420). This interest in antirealistic drama from the beginning of his career clearly indicates that Williams' later "presentational" works were not failed attempts at realism, as has repeatedly been suggested by critics, but rather the exploration of dramatic forms which had attracted him even during the height of his realistic period.

When *Camino Real* was produced in 1953, American audiences and critics were inhospitable to this experiment with freer forms, and so in his next offering, *Cat on a Hot Tin Roof* (1955), Williams returned to the more conventional style for which he was known. When he wrote *Camino Real* the theater was just being introduced to dramatic forms which broke with realistic conventions altogether in plays by writers such as Beckett, Ionesco, and Genet— plays which challenged realistic representations of language, time, space, and reality in an attempt to express the experience of metaphysical anguish in the face of an absurd and fragmented human condition. These new playwrights sought to confront and represent directly the meaninglessness of the human condition through the abandonment of traditional narrative plot and discursive language in favor of strikingly nonrational structures and a more minimalistic style of dialogue. They rebelled against realist attempts to order and represent the external world and instead presented reality as a subjective construct rather than as an objective truth which is perceived by the artist. Experimentation with theatrical conventions and the subjective representation of the artist's personal vision replaced mimesis in their works, as these artists were more interested in redefining what constitutes meaning through linguistic play and testing the limits of drama as performance. Because of this, their plays tend to be theme-centered rather than plot- or conflict-centered, a factor which constitutes the most marked break with the tradition of the "well-made play."

At the end of the 1940s and throughout the 1950s, these playwrights were setting the stage, so to speak, for a new kind of drama, one that deliberately questioned the nature of truth and reality primarily through exploring the notion that language interprets and constructs—rather than simply represents—the real. In Europe, Eugène Ionesco and Jean Genet were causing controversy throughout the 1950s with plays such as *The Bald Soprano, The Lesson*, and *The Balcony*, and Samuel Beckett's *Waiting For Godot* took Paris by storm in 1953 with its world premiere. While not an immediate success, *Godot* gradually became known throughout Europe for its highly unorthodox form and its controversial presentation of the futility of human existence. Translated into English by Beckett himself, the play was produced in London in 1955 and reached the United States in 1956. Although *Godot* bitterly disappointed its American audiences in its first production at the Miami Playhouse, it eventually reached Broadway and was generally acclaimed by the critical establishment. At this time British and American playwrights were beginning to catch on to the tide of experimental drama dominating the European theater scene, and during the late 1950s and early 1960s Harold Pinter's works were being introduced to London. *The Caretaker* eventually reached the States in 1961, and in the meantime Edward Albee was busy securing a place for what Esslin termed "The Theatre of the Absurd" in American drama. The director Herbert Blau returned from Europe in 1959 "convinced that crucial new directions in theater had been discovered on the continent, and that

American alternative theater, if it was to survive at all, would have to reckon with these new initiatives."[3] Blau's consequent productions of Beckett, Ionesco, and Genet in the United States, the translation of Antonin Artaud's *The Theater and Its Double* into English in 1958, and the powerful emergence of off-Broadway and off-off-Broadway in 1959 with the premiere of Albee's *The Zoo Story* and the Living Theater's pivotal production of Jack Gelber's *The Connection* (one of the first off-Broadway works to receive mainstream critical attention) promised drastic changes in the American theater. Williams enthusiastically embraced the work of these new alternative playwrights and wanted to be a part of the changes taking place in theater. Indeed, with the increasing popularity of writers such as Beckett, Pinter, and Albee, and the growing attention that off-Broadway theater was receiving, Williams felt that the 1960s would provide a hospitable arena for the unorthodox forms that had interested him for so long. While he claimed in a 1962 interview that he was "not crazy about Ionesco," he did say that he "loved" both Pinter and "Albee, best of our American playwrights."[4] In 1965, however, he told one interviewer that the theater of the absurd could not appeal to him since he "could never just make a joke out of human existence," and that he instead preferred "romantic fantasy" and, more vaguely, "very far-out plays."[5] Still, Williams believed that the new playwrights of the time such as Beckett, Gelber, Albee, and Pinter were "exploring the subtleties of human relationships that haven't been explored." He admired the "spareness" of their writing style which drove him "crazy with jealousy" and "enthralled" him at the theater.[6] Calling *The Caretaker* "a fabulous work," he said that "the play was about the thing that I've always pushed in my writing—that I've always felt was needed to be said over and over—that human relations are terrifyingly ambiguous. If you write a character that isn't ambiguous you are writing a false character, not a true one":

> I think the one beautiful and great thing about the new wave of playwrights is that they approach their subject matter with this kind of allusiveness. The whole attitude of this new wave of playwrights is not to preach, you know. Not to be dogmatic, to be provocatively allusive. And I think that's much truer.[7]

Rather than having his characters employ the signifiers typical of realistic dramaturgy to directly and articulately communicate their situations, thoughts, and emotions, Williams' later experiments—like the antirealistic plays of Beckett, Pinter, and Albee—keep action/movement to a minimum and reject an emphasis on the disclosures of plot. Instead, they focus more on the attempt to express and define experience which can be conveyed only through silence or evoked through fragmented, inarticulate moments of speech, in order to access the meaning that lies in the gaps in and between linguistic expressions. The overall dramaturgy of these later plays therefore differs greatly from realistic presentation and, consistent with these differences, language specifically is used differently. Characteristic of the experimental drama of the time, Williams' later works present and deconstruct the contradictions inherent in our constructed realities by prioritizing linguistic play over direct communication and exhibiting a focus on interiority which explores how the mind reinvents the past and translates experience into meaning.

In 1963, *The Milk Train Doesn't Stop Here Anymore*, a "sophisticated fairy tale" (5:3) which combines allegory, Kabuki theater, and realistic dramatic structures, was Williams' first major attempt since *Camino Real* to break away from predominantly realistic forms. Increasingly he began to move further away from realistic representation as he was determined to displace the emphasis on external reality in order to suggest a new perception of reality and experiment with alternative structures, many of which are evident in the later one-act plays included in the volume *Dragon Country* (1970). *I Can't Imagine Tomorrow* (1966, 1970) and *In the Bar of a Tokyo Hotel* (1969, 1970) present a linguistic reality which is rapidly deteriorating toward silence, while *The Mutilated* (1967) (which, like the early one-act *The Purification*, makes use of a Greek chorus) and *The Gnädiges Fräulein* (1967) are attempts at an absurdist dramatic style. Late full-length works such as *The Two-Character Play* (1969, 1973, 1976), *The Red Devil Battery Sign* (1975), *Clothes for a Summer Hotel* (1980, 1981), and *Something Cloudy, Something Clear* (1981), the last new play to be staged during Williams' lifetime, are representative of a potpourri of nonrealistic styles, as are later one-acts such as *Steps Must be Gentle* (1980), *Lifeboat Drill* (1981), and *Now the Cats With Jeweled Claws* (1981). *The Two-Character Play* is unmistakenly Beckettian in form: the characters are trapped in a linguistic nightmare in which the dialogue exists only to further the action and save them from silence rather than to communicate a determinate meaning. The fragmented, minimalistic language of *Lifeboat Drill* and *Now the Cats With Jeweled Claws* similarly exhibits the breakdown of rational expression, while *Clothes for a Summer Hotel* and *Steps Must be*

Gentle contain elements which identify them as Williams' "ghost plays" in the spirit of Strindberg. *The Red Devil Battery Sign* ends with a gesture toward surrealism, and *Something Cloudy, Something Clear* features dream images, mime, and dance.

I Can't Imagine Tomorrow (1966), *In the Bar of a Tokyo Hotel* (1969), and *The Two-Character Play* (first version performed 1967) are the most successful examples of the complex and interesting goals of Williams' later phase, and they will be my focus for the rest of this chapter. Before exploring them individually, however, it is necessary to provide an overview of what exactly Williams was trying to represent in these plays and the means of representation he employed. In distinguishing these plays from those of his early years, the dramaturgical departures from realism in terms of action, language, character, and plot must be examined. These later plays draw attention to a consciousness of performance and emphasize the ambiguity resulting from a language which inadequately expresses ideas and emotions. They do not seek to reproduce the illusionistic drama of closure/(dis)closure and the reestablishment of order that realism embraces; rather, they deliberately avoid the "slice of life" illusion, reproduction of realistic speech patterns through referential language, consistent character psychology and development, and the kind of linear narrative plot that characterizes realistic drama.

While Williams' realistic plays sought to portray characters as complex human beings ("ordinary people") who attempt to express their thoughts and feelings regarding difficult life situations, characters in the later antirealistic plays are not characters in the realistic sense of the word, but often are themselves representations of a particular idea, emotion, or theme, following a more subjective point of view. This representation of character, which often seeks to directly represent the nonrational paradoxes of the human psyche, is in marked contrast to the characterological model of the Method, the style of acting commonly associated with the more realistic plays of Tennessee Williams and the popular American cinema. The Method strives for a portrayal of character through creation from "within," employing the actor's own imagination and intuition to produce the illusion of a complex "personality"—a seamless unity of psychic coherence—whose motivations are exposed and explored.

In his earlier work Williams was essentially calling for human tolerance for those sensitive individuals who are forced to exist in a reality permeated with violence. The only successful escape from this harsh reality was possible through fantasy and a rejection of the world. In *Stairs to the Roof* (1942), for example, the protagonists literally remove themselves from this world as they climb a stairway to the roof to meet an old man with a flowing white beard who whisks them to another planet to begin a new life. Aside from physical flight, the only other means of escape featured in the early plays is a symbolic rejection of the world through madness. Otherwise, there is destruction and death. The most sophisticated of Williams' experimental plays during his later period such as *I Can't Imagine Tomorrow, In the Bar of a Tokyo Hotel*, and *The Two-Character Play* still focus on a desire to escape—here not only from a disturbing existence in which the characters are trapped, but also from a dialogue which frustrates and alienates them. However, suspicious of the language which has become their prison, they have resigned themselves to the fact that the only escape is silence and death, and they don't even seem to hope for anything to save or protect them. The panic, fear, and loneliness they experience postpone "the end," however, and the characters have no choice but to "go on" in an endless cycle of representation which is linguistically and philosophically fragmented. In these plays Williams is representing a private psychological world in which the characters are trapped within themselves rather than within a particular situation, as was the case with Blanche DuBois or Tom Wingfield, for example. In the later works there is no place to which or from which to escape.

Williams' attempt in the later plays to locate and directly represent an absolute, intangible reality apart from an external reality which he once described as "the everyday humdrum world"[8] indicates a different subject of representation than we saw in his early work. While the ultimate goal of getting closer to a truth which exists outside of language is no different from the goal he claimed for his early realistic plays, in *I Can't Imagine Tomorrow, In the Bar of a Tokyo Hotel*, and *The Two-Character Play* he seeks to reach that goal primarily through the representation and exploration of the psychological process rather than through the representation of human interaction. All three of these later plays represent an emotion—predominantly fear—rather than a social situation. In his later work Williams sought to represent this intangible emotion which had plagued him throughout his career. The fear of confinement, of insanity, of loneliness, and of the artist losing himself in his own creation mirror Williams' own fears which were presented strongly as *themes* in his earlier work, but not represented directly in the mise-en-scène and the form of the dialogue.

As Williams' subject of representation changed in his later plays, his mode of representation—the use of language, the construction of character, and the manipulation of mise-en-scène—had to shift away from realism in order to accommodate that change. But unlike many of the playwrights and performance groups of the 1960s and 1970s, such as Jean-Claude Van Itallie or the Living Theatre, Williams did not turn to a form of theater which rejected an emphasis on language altogether and instead centered on the physical or "vaudevillian" method of presentation, with its focus on the body, the improvised moment, and theater as ritualistic space. In Williams' later plays (with the exception, perhaps, of the one-act plays *The Mutilated* and *The Gnädiges Fräulein*) language continued to be an important aspect of his overall dramaturgy. However, while both Williams' early and late work were committed to the exploration of language, his presentation of language was changing in the 1960s. He turned away from the long poetic speeches which—along with the construction of psychologically complex realistic characters with whom an audience could identify—had been his trademark, and attempted to move toward a more minimalistic approach to dramatic language in the plays of his later period. He began to rely less on language as a direct, reliable expression of truth and more on the silences, pauses, and indirect implications that lie beyond the capacity of verbal representation in order to express the idea that reality could not be articulated—a central goal of the experimental art which exploded in the wake of the new dramatists. In a 1949 dialogue of homage to the painter Bram van Velde, Beckett challenges the assumption of realistic representation that the artist has something in particular to express and succeeds in expressing it in his work. He describes this sense of obligation as frustrated by incapacity, and speaks of a new art, the preference of which will be "The expression that there is nothing to express, nothing with which to express, nothing from which to express, no power to express, no desire to express, together with the obligation to express."[9] Williams' later plays make use of a dialogue which focuses on the subtleties of linguistic play and punning language, creating gaps in the attempts to communicate meaning as, simultaneously, these gaps become the meaning. In his later years Williams remained a "poet" of the theater, but his poetry lay more in the incompleteness of communication than in direct expression. He began to feel very strongly that "poetry doesn't have to be words, you see. In the theatre it can be situations, it can be silences."[10]

In Williams' earlier plays descriptive dialogue and narrative situation are used to express the characters' sense of isolation and their frustration in communicating their emotions and ideas. In *Orpheus Descending* (1958), for example, Williams supports Val's statement that "We're all of us sentenced to solitary confinement inside our own skins, for life!" (3:271) with the development of the play's action, its "story." Ironically, Val eloquently communicates the incommunicability of ideas and emotions between human beings through his language. Similarly, Tom's confession to Amanda that "You say there's so much in your heart that you can't describe to me. That's true of me too. There's so much in my heart that I can't describe to *you!*" (1:173) is expressed through language rather than the silence it would presume to call for. In the later works, however, Williams actually illustrates Val's philosophy through the use of a fragmented and nondiscursive dialogue. The inability to express human experience is represented through the *form* of the minimalistic, repetitive dialogue (or silence), rather than expressed directly in the content of the language. In the best of Williams' later plays, meaning is not located or pinned down; while fragmented sentences and staccato dialogue contribute to the lack of a single, stable meaning, simultaneously the language is deliberately overdetermined (often through puns or layered meanings) in order to emphasize its inherent ambiguity and inadequacy in expressing truth. Rather than simply incorporating antirealistic devices that would help enhance the realistic goals of his plays as he did in his early work, Williams' most sophisticated later work exploits the position of nonrealistic theater that the referential codes of realistic presentation can never actually represent the real on stage, precisely because these codes are always only a representation of themselves. Bigsby comments on this aspect of antirealistic theater, writing that in much drama of the 1960s language, especially, "was to be liberated from its role as signifier. It was to be broken down into sound units, fragmented into syllables, explored for its sonorities, tonalities."[11]

Williams' interest in the fragmented dialogue that focuses on the paradox of the inexpressibility of human expression emerges at moments in some of his early one-act plays, but he expands these experiments with language in his later one-acts. *I Can't Imagine Tomorrow* is essentially a work which deals with the theme of pathological human dependence expressed through a fragmented dialogue which illustrates the inability of one character to finish a sentence without the other. As in *In the Bar of a Tokyo Hotel* and

The Two-Character Play, in *I Can't Imagine Tomorrow* Williams has apparently divided himself into two characters—called "One" and "Two" in this play—who depend on each other for survival, leading critics to focus often on the "excessively personal" and autobiographical aspects of the play as opposed to its autonomy as an art form. Although *I Can't Imagine Tomorrow* is written for a man and a woman, a 1989 production by the Mason Gross School of the Arts at the Levin Theater in New Brunswick, New Jersey, cast two men in the roles of One and Two. This gesture encouraged a very literal autobiographical interpretation of the play, and indeed in both this play and *In the Bar of a Tokyo Hotel* there are elements of Williams' relationship with Frank Merlo. In *Tokyo Hotel* the relationship between the dying artist and his wife is decaying after fourteen years (7:45), the precise duration of the relationship between Williams and Merlo. Williams often claimed that Merlo's death greatly affected his writing: "Frank had a great influence on my life as an artist. After his death there was a drastic change in my style of writing."[12] He once said that Frank "kept his door locked" during his illness and "didn't want anyone near him. He was like a cat—they withdraw when they're dying."[13] In *Can't Imagine,* the emotionally strong but physically decaying One, like Frank, shuns companionship on her deathbed: "Sorry. I have to be alone here" (7:149). And Two's "difficulty in speaking" (7:134) mirrors Williams' own "inability to talk to people" after Frank's death.[14] After responding to a question about *Can't Imagine* and *Tokyo Hotel* in a 1969 interview with Dan Isaac just before his breakdown, Williams, after a silent pause, told the interviewer: "I don't complete many sentences these days."[15]

In *I Can't Imagine Tomorrow,* One tells a story about a "small man" who goes to the house of Death and shouts loudly until he is finally let in, despite the fact that he has arrived twenty years too early (7:143–44). One tells Two that this is his story: "You made it up. You've been making it up for a long time now. It's time to send it out for publication. Don't you think so?" (7:144). In a 1981 letter, Williams told Gregory Mosher, artistic director of the Goodman Theatre at the time, that this speech in *Can't Imagine* "perfectly described his life since the death of Frank Merlo almost twenty years earlier."[16]

I Can't Imagine Tomorrow does not, however, depend on Williams' autobiography for its significance. This play is similar to both *In the Bar of a Tokyo Hotel* and *The Two-Character Play* in its representation of a symbiotic pair of characters who must confront the impending threat of insanity through the loss of a stable center of truth, a loss that is represented by a fragmented language which seems disconnected from the character who is speaking it. However, while in the two later plays both characters are moving toward silence and fragmentation as a result of their frustration with being trapped in an essentially meaningless language, in *I Can't Imagine Tomorrow* one character ("One") still retains the ability and the desire to express herself in language, while the other ("Two"), who had always found it difficult "To put what I think and feel into speech" (7:140), speaks very little and often in incomplete sentences. Therefore, the two characters in *I Can't Imagine Tomorrow* can be seen as representing a transition from the realistic language and mode of representation employed in the early plays toward the breakdown of linguistic expression which Williams seeks to represent in the later works.

In this play, One and Two, a woman and a man respectively, repeat the same empty routine together every evening in order to pass time and divert their attention from their fear of silence, death, and change. This routine forms the cornerstone of their relationship; One tells Two: "I see you every evening. It wouldn't be evening without you and the card game and the news on TV" (7:134). The fear of change is so paralyzing that Two, a junior high school teacher, has presumably lost his job since he has been unable to meet his classes for a week. Williams has therefore provided a realistic basis for Two's retreat into silence, as Two even attempts to see a therapist for his problem, claiming that the situation was "desperate" and "urgent" since he could no longer address his classes, and that "there was only one person" that he could still talk to "a little" (7:136). The characters' situation is rapidly approaching Beckett's world of decay, mutual dependence, repetition, and frustration, but One is struggling to resist that fate:

> Every evening you have a frightened, guilty expression. I always say, "Oh, it's you," and you always say, "Yes, it's me." . . . We have to repeat the ritual, oh, it's you and yes, it's me, there's almost nothing else said, at least nothing else worth saying. I force myself to carry on a sort of monologue. . . . And I tell you things I've told you so often before I'm ashamed to repeat them. But I have to repeat them or we'd just sit together in unbearable silence, yes, intolerable silence. (7:140)

Two's fear is mainly a pervasive dread, with no known origin or rational cause other than simply being alive. As early as 1950,

Williams attempted to explain this "Sense of Dreadfulness" in his introduction to Carson McCullers' *Reflections in a Golden Eye*:

the true sense of dread is not a reaction to anything sensible or visible or even, strictly, materially, *knowable*. But rather it's a kind of spiritual intuition of something almost too incredible and shocking to talk about, which underlies the whole so-called thing. It is the incommunicable something that we shall have to call *mystery* which is so inspiring of dread among . . . modern artists.[17]

Despite One's encouragement, Two is unable to locate and articulate effectively the fear that paralyzes him. One prompts him:

Take this piece of paper and this pencil and write me the first thing that comes into your mind. Quick. Don't stop to think. [Two scratches something on the paper.] Good. Let me see what you wrote. "I love you and I'm afraid."—What are you afraid of? Quick. Write it down. [He scratches something on the paper again. She snatches the paper from him.] "Changes."—Do you mean changes in yourself or in me or changes in circumstances affecting our lives? Quick, write it down, don't think. [He writes again.] "Everything. All." (7:140)

Two can barely complete sentences by himself throughout the play, and it is the prompting from One which furthers the dialogue. During these exchanges the dialogue takes on a staccato rhythm, and the content often deals with madness and breakdown:

Two. There's always—

One. What?

Two. Got to be something, as long as—

One. Yes, as long as we live.

Two. Today. Today I did go.

One. To the clinic?

Two. Yes. There.

One. What did you tell them? What did they tell you?

Two. I only talked to the girl, the—

One. Receptionist?

Two. Yes, she gave me a paper, a—

One. An application, a—

Two. Questionnaire to—

One. Fill out?

(7:135)

Silences and pauses figure strongly in *I Can't Imagine Tomorrow*, as communication is breaking down. The first few stage directions open the play with a "strangely prolonged silence, during which neither moves" followed by "another strange pause" shortly afterward (7:133).

While mentally and emotionally One appears to be the stronger of the two characters, physically she is breaking down just as Two is linguistically breaking down. Two is approaching the silence which will free him from the prisonhouse of language through a "living" silence—madness—but One is moving toward the alternative—death. She can no longer eat anything, won't leave the house or change her clothes, and experiences frequent spasms of pain which make it difficult for her to climb the stairs to the bedroom, despite her determination: "I'll go on up to my bedroom in a while, even if I have to crawl up the rest of the stairs" (7:149). One needs Two for physical survival just as he needs her for emotional survival, but now that she is apparently dying, she encourages Two to form new acquaintances:

> I'm going upstairs, after all. I can still get up them if I take my time about it and hold onto the banisters. . . . And as for you, don't forget my advice to strike up some new acquaintances. It doesn't have to be at the soda fountain, it could be at a bar. Say something to somebody. That's my advice, but I can see it's wasted. (7:146)

Two is both unwilling and unable "to strike up some new acquaintances" precisely because of his detachment from a world which insists that he must "Say something to somebody" in order to experience validation of that world and of his own identity. His fear is a fear of annihilation as he approaches the silence that signifies his rejection of a reality which is both constructed in and constructed by language.

While in *I Can't Imagine Tomorrow* Williams employs essentially realistic structures of communication which are rapidly breaking down, the fragmented language that characterizes *In the Bar of a Tokyo Hotel* exhibits a dialogue which has moved even further toward silence and does not even attempt to reproduce realistic communication. Sentences are rarely finished and experience is presented as fragmented and cyclical, rather than as the teleological, linear experience of realism:

> *Miriam.* I could have you committed to a.
>
> *Mark.* It wouldn't be the first time you've tried to put me away, without.

Miriam. Without what?

Mark. Without considering the.

Miriam. What?

Mark. The consequences. I never could stand confinement.

Miriam. When a person needs help.

(7:24)

Much of the dialogue in *Tokyo Hotel* takes this truncated form, and it is interesting to note that the fragmented sentences usually end with periods rather than dashes, indicating that the character who is speaking is finished speaking, rather than being interrupted. It is therefore the thoughts as well as the sentences that are incomplete. Rational linguistic structures have, for the most part, broken down, and we are outside the constructed boundaries of sanity. The language of *Tokyo Hotel* is the language of madness, and it is the omnipresent fear of madness that dominates its atmosphere.

Williams has called this work the "first full statement of [his] darker vision," and it was the last play he wrote before his nervous breakdown and subsequent hospitalization in the psychiatric division of Barnes Hospital in 1969.[18] "At the time of *In the Bar of a Tokyo Hotel*," Williams said in 1975, "I was just approaching the collapse."[19] Mark and Miriam of *Tokyo Hotel* are a married couple who could be said to represent the two sides of Williams that were struggling with each other for sanity throughout the 1960s and beyond. Williams himself has said that "the couple, the artist and his wife in that play, were two sides of one person,"[20] and this idea is also effectively articulated in the text of the play:

Miriam. —Are we two people, Mark, or are we—

Mark. [with the force of dread] Stop there! [She lifts her hands to her face, but the words continue through it.]

Miriam. Two sides of!

Mark. Stop!

Miriam. One! An artist inhabiting the body of a compulsive—

Mark. Bitch!

Miriam. Call me that, but remember that you're denouncing a side of yourself, denied by you!

(7:30)

Mark, the perceptive and sensitive artist whose highly emotional nature and excessive devotion to his art renders him exhausted and barely capable of daily survival, is on the verge of insanity, constantly falling down throughout the play. Like Two in *I Can't Imagine Tomorrow*, he can barely complete a sentence on his own. He is overcome with a sense of fear and dread, and lacks the energy to fight the demons of insanity (Shannon's "spooks" or Hannah's "blue devils" in *Night of the Iguana*). Mark can certainly be read as a portrait of Williams during the 1960s, before he was committed to Barnes hospital. Williams later acknowledged that by the end of 1968 (the year he began writing *Tokyo Hotel*), he "was writing . . . under speed" and "falling down a lot."[21] Maureen Stapleton has said that by 1965 Williams' addiction to pills was so bad that "we'd enter a restaurant and before Tenn had had even one drink, he'd fall down. After a while he was always falling down."[22]

Like Williams, Mark is branching out toward new forms in his art, but feels lost in his latest creations and is unable to control his work, despite his determination: "In the beginning, a new style of work can be stronger than you, but you learn to control it. It has to be controlled. You learn to control it" (7:21). Mark struggles to communicate the loss of any distinctness between himself and his art that he has come to feel, but the fear and terror associated with the "oneness" he experiences paralyzes him:

> *Mark.* I've understood the *intimacy* that should, that should, that has to exist between the, the—painter and the—I! it! Now it turned to me, or I turned to it, no division between us at all anymore! The one-ness, the!
>
> *Miriam:* Are you hysterical? I'll get the bell captain to get you a tape recorder to preserve your delirious ravings. Play them back to yourself and you might be as shocked as I am by the.
>
> *Mark.* Images in!
>
> *Miriam.* Recorded.
>
> *Mark.* There was always a sense of division till! Gone! Now absolute one-ness with!
>
> (7:17)

And later,

> *Mark.* When I say that I'm terrified of the new canvasses, you think I'm exaggerating.

Miriam. Not at all in the least.

Mark. No separation between myself and.

(7:21)

Once when asked what his interpretation of this play was, Williams replied to an interviewer: "The theme of creation."[23]

Mark's wife, Miriam, is a hard-edged, unsentimental, and sexually predatory antidote to the excessively sensitive Mark. Since Mark's emotional instability and physical dependence render him ineffective as a companion or sexual partner, Miriam pursues life through promiscuous sex, seeking refuge from her loneliness and her fear of death in the companionship of anonymous encounters:

> *Miriam.* Some women grow suddenly old. They go to bed young, well, reasonably young women and when they wake up in the morning and go to the mirror, they face—what?—A specter! . . . Themselves, yes, but not young, reasonably young, women, no, not any more! Oh, they continue to pursue, if they are like me, the pursuit would continue! But the desired stranger would offer them no more than a minute of his time. A glance in a glistening bar. And I fear death, I know it would have to remove, wrench, tear!—the bracelets off my arms. . . . To be old, suddenly old—*no!* Unacceptable to me on any terms! Terror, yes, I could say terror! (7:37)

Just as the dying artist lost in his creation and "falling down a lot" mirrors Williams' fears and behavior throughout the 1960s, the lustful predator seeking shelter from fear and death through sexuality mirrors a side of Williams that he readily admitted and portrayed through his characters. In 1952, discussing the influences involved in his upbringing (his maternal grandfather was an Episcopal clergyman and his paternal ancestry boasted pioneer Tennessee stock), he wrote that "Roughly there was a combination of Puritan and Cavalier strains in my blood which may be accountable for the conflicting impulses I often represent in the people I write about."[24] Miriam is sexually aggressive and straightforward, and the Barman in fact spends most of his time avoiding her sexual advances. She has no illusions concerning her predatory impulses and insists that she doesn't "like objects that disguise their true nature" (7:19).

The "conflicting impulses" represented in Mark and Miriam are not only personifications of Williams' own divided nature; they also echo the familiar Lawrencian paradigm that has appeared in Williams' work before: the equation of the life force with sexuality, struggling to overcome the sickly death instinct which is a rejection of the sexual impulse. In a note to his one-act play about D. H. Lawrence, *I Rise in Flame, Cried the Phoenix* (1951), Williams writes that

> Lawrence felt the mystery and power of sex, as the primal life urge, and was the life-long adversary of those who wanted to keep the subject locked away in the cellars of prudery. Much of his work is chaotic and distorted by tangent obsessions, such as his insistence upon the woman's subservience to the male, but all in all his work is probably the greatest modern monument to the dark roots of creation. (7:56)

Blanche and Stanley in *Streetcar*, Alma and John in *Summer and Smoke*, Serafina and Mangiacavallo in *The Rose Tattoo*, Maggie and Brick in *Cat*, all perform elements of this struggle. *In the Bar of a Tokyo Hotel*, however, handles this Lawrencian split in a radically different manner from its predecessors. The most obvious difference is that, unlike the autonomous and complex characters in the earlier plays who were able to stand apart from the pair, Mark and Miriam are a symbiotic unit, dependent on each other beyond the level of emotional security or psychological tension expected from characters in accordance with realistic principles—they are, as Williams reminds us, "two sides of one person."[25] But while there are certainly both autobiographical clues and extratextual associations which may be applied as the "key" to Williams' representation of Mark and Miriam's contrary natures, when taken in the play's full context the central aspect of their symbiosis is independent of these hints, as it lies in the fragmented and degenerating language which binds them together—making them linguistically codependent and blurring the boundaries between self and other.

Of the three plays I deal with in this chapter, this one is arguably the weakest in terms of overall dramatic tension and effective dialogue, but Williams' attempt here at expressing a reality that cannot be expressed in discursive language, but rather only through the degenerated form which the language takes, is admirable. Moreover, in addition to the interesting experiments with truncated and fragmented language, the play's portrait of the divided artist, struggling with himself and his art for sanity, make this a play worth exploring. It incorporates all the frustration, confusion, fear, and paranoia of the artist who is losing control of himself and his work and yet is unable to escape either, since both must be defined and articulated by a language which, by its very nature, cannot be stabilized. Once the artist realizes that the chain of signifiers making up language constantly resists any determinate meaning which could lead to a stable truth, all that language has constructed—the self, relationships, meaning, and artistic creation—dissolves and fragments. This revelation appears to be precisely the "darker vision" that Williams felt the need, ironically, to try and articulate.

The most impressive example of Williams' departure from realism toward a more antirealistic drama is his frequently revised *The Two-Character Play*, first staged in London in December 1967, then rewritten and presented under the title *Out Cry* in Chicago in July 1971, reworked once again for a New York production in March 1973, and yet again (with the original title restored) for another New York production in August 1975.[26] Williams was convinced that this play was a major creative work, and he once said that he "never stopped working on it."[27] His longtime friend Maria St. Just notes that *Out Cry* was "so important a play" for Williams that "he always referred to it as OUT CRY—of all his plays, the only title that he *always* typed in capital letters."[28]

The Two-Character Play incorporates the experiments with language, character, and setting that Williams introduced in *I Can't Imagine Tomorrow* and *In the Bar of a Tokyo Hotel*—as well as, as Roger Boxill argues, even earlier one-acts:

> Despite its Pirandellian form, *Two-Character* is a logical outgrowth of the one-act *I Can't Imagine Tomorrow* (1966), a strangely vague and intimate duologue that is itself anticipated by the earlier one-act *Talk to Me Like the Rain and Let Me Listen* (1953) and even by the closing exchanges of *The Lady of Larkspur Lotion* long before it.[29]

The Two-Character Play focuses on the symbiotic relationship between two characters, Clare and Felice, a brother and sister who often "have the same thought at the same time" (5:366). These characters are apparently actors in a play-within-a-play of the same name, and the boundaries between their metatheatrical performances and their performances in Williams' drama are blurred. In his biography of his brother, Dakin Williams describes the play in this way:

> There is no realistic setting, the sets are all built out of words. A brother and sister, Felice and Clare, are living, like recluses, in their family's house. Their mother and father have been killed, perhaps, as the sister says, by a housebreaker (we assume this is not true), or that "father killed mother and himself" (possibly true), or even

conceivably (we're never sure) the two of them may have done it, or perhaps they only *thought* they might have.

Their relationship is—incestuous? Well, perhaps not physically—or is it? They are insane? Well, they know all about *State Haven*, the local asylum; they have surely been inmates there. They have no money, and no way of making it, and now almost no food, and are terrified to go on, and they will probably just stay in the house and starve.[30]

Or probably not. We never know. As for the brother and sister living in their family's house, this is uncertain as well. They seem to be living in a theater, and the family's house is only the set of the play they're performing. But we're never sure of that either. Disclosure here is minimal and ambiguous. Nothing is certain or stable in this play. In response to Clare's demand of *"Restoration of—order!"* Felice asks, "What order?" (5:313). Clare desires the reestablishment of "Rational, rational!" constructs (5:313), but we are not in the realm of the "rational" structures that Clare (as well as an audience expecting realistic drama) requires.

The Two-Character Play does not cater to the central illusions of realism, but rather stretches and transforms the boundaries of realistic conventions, playing with the notions of realistic space, consistent and logical character, (dis)closure, and the re-establishment of a dominant order. Williams "teases" the audience with the expectation of the unfolding of a stable narrative core, yet each "disclosure" reveals only more uncertainty. Moreover, the language of the play is strikingly unlike the long, discursive passages of Williams' early work. Here Williams clearly displays the "gun-fire dialogue" he said he was moving towards in 1962. In this play both the inadequacies (represented through silences) and overdetermined quality of language (represented through linguistic play) are emphasized over its signifying powers and its supposed access to truth. For the first time in a major play, Williams uses puns to draw attention to the deliberately ambiguous meanings that language generates. The opening line, in fact, is a pun: "To play with fear is to play with fire" (5:309). *The Two-Character Play* is a powerful contribution to the artistic and philosophical climate of the 1960s, since it is arguable that this play goes beyond the work of avant-garde dramatists such as Beckett and Pinter by combining their exploitation of linguistic and dramatic irony with the poetic nuances that distinguished Williams' work during the 1940s and 1950s. Since both poetry and puns rely on the conscious overdetermination of language,

Williams' text is both lyrically and ironically overdetermined, an achievement which makes *The Two-Character Play* both indulgently poignant and starkly conscious of linguistic paradoxes.

The theme that dominates this work is fear, and in one sense the *New York Times* was right in calling it a "one-character . . . monologue."[31] Clare and Felice are less characters in the realistic sense of the term than they are representations of the psychological state of fear and panic. Even their names, as has been pointed out by several critics, are ambiguous in terms of gender; both the characters and the names assigned to them could be interchanged without altering the play significantly. The central object onstage is "a (papier-mâché) statue of a giant, pedestaled, which has a sinister look" (5:308) and contributes to the "unreality" of the play's atmosphere. The statue represents fear, and it looms over the characters throughout the play as a reminder to us of where they are, inside "a mind approaching collapse" (stage direction, 5:308). Williams makes a point of saying that the setting must "suggest the disordered images of a mind approaching collapse . . . [and] correspondingly, the phantasmagoria of the nightmarish world that all of us live in at present, not just the subjective but the true world with all its dismaying shapes and shadows" (5:308). The atmosphere is that of a dream—simultaneously horrifying and beautiful—and the boundaries of realistic space and time no longer hold. When the play opens, the appearance of Clare is made dreamlike and "phantasmagoric": "CLARE appears in the Gothic door to the backstage area. There is a ghostly spill of light in the doorway and she has an apparitional look about her" (5:310). Madness becomes *externalized* and *amplified* in *The Two-Character Play* through the setting. The madness is everywhere—it *is* the real—as the representation of the mind becomes the play. This is a very different intention from an early play such as *Streetcar*, for example, where there is a distinct separation of subjective psychology and objective reality, as in the case of Blanche's madness, which exists only in her "mind," not in the "real world." This separation also exists in *Cat on a Hot Tin Roof*, where Williams claims that rather than trying to explore "the solution of one man's psychological problem," he is "trying to catch the true quality of experience in a group of people, that cloudy, flickering, evanescent—fiercely charged!—interplay of live human beings in the thundercloud of a common crisis" (3:114). With his later work Williams departed from his desire to represent the macroscopic in terms of social situations, and moved toward a kind of representation which merges the microscopic and the macroscopic—the direct representation of the individual psyche with its fears and limitless distortions is simultaneously the "world" of the play.

While fear, isolation, and loneliness were almost always present in Williams' earlier drama as themes embedded in the plot, in his later drama Williams attempted to represent these psychological states directly through the setting and the fragmented structure of the dialogue. Since a major part of Williams' fame as a dramatist rested on his brilliant and complex construction of memorable characters, his abandonment of the focus on realistic character was often (wrongly) seen as a failure on his part to live up to his former accomplishments. What Bigsby says of Edward Albee can be applied to Williams as well in this context:

> since his concern was increasingly with consciousness, the way in which we constitute the real, it was likely that he would focus less on character as social and psychological fact than as construction, as artifice; less on plot as sequence of event than as performance; less on language as speech act than as a means to give shape and form to experience.[32]

The dialogue of *The Two-Character Play* exists mostly for diversion, to subdue the panic and fear of silence and death that the characters feel. In 1971 Williams remarked to an interviewer: "I think I've always been somewhat preoccupied with [death]. It appears in my plays as an excessively recurring theme."[33] Discussing how discourse is used to hold "death . . . at arm's length" in the plays of Eugene O'Neill, Bigsby cites Foucault's observation that "speaking so as not to die is a task . . . as old as the word."[34] We see this connection in Williams' play from the beginning, as Felice's opening monologue contains a meditation on death as the only release from fear:

> Fear! The fierce little man with the drum inside the rib cage. Yes, compared to fear grown to panic which has no—what?—limits, at least none short of consciousness blowing out and not reviving again, compared to that, no other emotion a living, feeling creature is capable of having, not even love or hate, is comparable in—what?—force?—magnitude? (5:309)

While this passage illustrates the inability of language to express emotion accurately and adequately, its inarticulateness is, at the same time, philosophically poetic. The fragmentation of expression indicated by the dashes, the question marks, and the search for the "right words" is balanced by the very lyrical and articulate metaphoric moments. The stammering panic expressed directly in the form of the monologue exhibits the slipperiness and incompletion of language, while the descriptions of fear as the "fierce little man with the drum inside the rib cage" and death as "consciousness blowing out and not reviving again" are characteristic of the gift for poetry that helped establish Williams' early career.

The fear which pervades *The Two-Character Play* is, like the fear that Two experiences in *I Can't Imagine Tomorrow*, the modernist "Sense of Dreadfulness" that Williams attempted to describe in his introduction to Carson McCullers' *Reflections in a Golden Eye*. It is this sense that Williams repeatedly seeks to represent in the later plays. Often it is related to confinement or isolation, to being trapped and alone:

> *Clare.* We have no communication with the front of the house? [She coughs and spits]
>
> *Felice.* None.
>
> *Clare.* You mean we're—?
>
> *Felice.* Isolated. Completely.
>
> (5:318)

Clare can't even bring herself to utter the word "isolated," as if expressing the condition in language would give it a determined reality. But Felice undermines Clare's sense that the word creates reality by reminding her, as Williams reminds his audience, that the gaps of silence—that which is not said—is just as powerful as language, if not more so:

> *Clare.* You shouldn't have spoken that word! Confined! That word is not in the—
>
> *Felice.* Oh. A prohibited word. When a word can't be used, when it's prohibited its silence increases its size. It gets larger and larger till it's so enormous that no house can hold it.
>
> *Clare.* Then say the word, over and over, you—*perverse monster,* you!
>
> (5:338)

The characters' fear of confinement seems to be even greater than that of isolation, as confinement is the condition which is forbidden utterance—it is the "prohibited word." Clare's desire to stick to the "script" (we presume she was about to say "That word is not in the *script*") points to a desire for the order that she has craved (5:313); it is an attempt to control reality through controlling the language that creates it.

The play opens with Felice "slowly, reflectively, writing" (5:309), consciously negotiating the language of his presentation. Throughout this work, a style of dialogue which explores the paradox of linguistic presentation is substituted for the elaborate metaphors of the early works, as Williams illustrates the instability of language through linguistic play:

> *Felice.* Have you got an *"upper"?*
>
> *Clare.* One for emergency, but—
>
> *Felice.* I think you'd better *drop it.*
>
> (5:312, emphasis mine)

> *Felice.* [Overlapping.] What I know is I play with a freaked out, staggering—
>
> *Clare.* [Overlapping.] Well, play with yourself, you long-haired son of a mother!
>
> *Felice.* [Overlapping.] Your voice is thick, slurred, you've picked up—vulgarisms of—gutters!
>
> *Clare.* [Overlapping.] What you pick up is stopped at the desk of any decent hotel.
>
> (5:315)

The language here is deliberately ironic and punning, and creates a tension which makes communication complex and ambiguous. Bigsby writes that the play depends on an irony which cannot be transcended, only performed. The dramatic tension no longer comes "from the space which opens up between illusion and the real," as it once did in the early work. Instead, it is "generated by the language itself, brittle, incapable of sustaining communication."[35]

This "space" to which Bigsby refers ("which opens up between illusion and the real") does not, in fact, exist in this play, for in it Williams deconstructs the concept of reality, leaving the characters with no stable, locatable condition on which to rely. The boundaries between reality and illusion/fiction are blurred from the beginning as Clare and Felice are drawn into the play-within-a-play, losing any well-defined sense of where the "fictional" play ends and their "real life" narrative begins. While Blanche DuBois was taken away to a mental asylum, it seems that Clare and Felice are already trapped in their asylum, which is also simultaneously a house, a theater, and a prison. The clear-cut distinction between Blanche's fantasy world and the realm of reality in which the characters interact in *A Streetcar Named Desire* is absent from *The Two-Character Play*, and in terms of the physical realm as well this is a play which resists realistic space:

> *Felice.* I realize, now, that the house has turned to a prison.
>
> *Clare.* I know it's a prison, too, but it's one that isn't strange to us.
> (5:354)

> *Clare.* So it's a prison, this last theatre of ours?
>
> *Felice.* It would seem to be one.
>
> *Clare.* (objectively, now): I've always suspected that theatres are prisons for players . . .
>
> *Felice.* Finally, yes. And for writers of plays.
> (5:364)

While Williams in these lines is making a comment on the nature of language and repetition in the theater as a continuing cycle of representation which traps the player (and the playwright) in the dialogue, the breakdown of the distinction between a realm of illusion (theaters, mental asylums) and a realm of "reality" is central to this drama.[36] Clare and Felice are acting a double role, both in the play and in the play-within-a-play. Boxill writes that

> Whether Clare and Felice are actors playing themselves or asylum inmates playing actors playing themselves, the play and the play-within-the-play work together in complementary fashion to show the brother and the sister locked within an unbreakable circle of dread and pain.[37]

Bigsby argues that the fact that Clare and Felice are actors is central to the drama:

> Apparently abandoned by their company, there is nothing for them to do but speak their lines with diminishing confidence, perform their lives even if that performance has been drained of meaning. The audience, if it ever existed, disappears, leaving them to enact a play, apparently based on their own lives, in an empty theatre. They have no alternative but to continue their performance though, denied an audience, they are denied equally the significance which that audience might have been prepared to grant to that performance. . . . The

theatre is the condition of their existence; acting the only verification of their being.[38]

There are several references in *The Two-Character Play* to being "lost in the play" (5:317, 318, 367), a phrase which draws attention to the use of both "play" and "lost" as central puns. The characters must lose themselves both in the act of performance—the play—and in the linguistic play that saves them from the silence they fear. Moreover, they are "lost" not only in the sense that they are totally absorbed in their activity, but also in the sense that they are dislocated, disoriented, unsure of their whereabouts. All they have is the play, but the dialogue of *The Two-Character Play*—like that of *I Can't Imagine Tomorrow* and *In the Bar of a Tokyo Hotel*—is heading rapidly toward a silence which the characters both desire and resist. However, it is precisely the performance of the dialogue that defines their existence and wards off the silence, enabling Clare and Felice to "go on."

Although at one point Williams changed the title of *The Two-Character Play* to *Out Cry*, restoring the original title was in keeping with his apparent purpose, since the play-within-the-play is also called *The Two-Character Play*, and the identities of the two titles help blur the boundaries between fiction and reality all the more. Moreover, in all versions of Williams' play Clare and Felice are the names of both the play's two characters and of the characters they play in the internal drama. The dissolution of constructed boundaries is taken yet a step further with Williams' choice of these essentially unisex names which blur gender distinctions. "Even the characters' names," Bigsby reminds us, "support a sexual ambiguity which is rooted in more than Williams's own sensibility. The androgynous is itself an embodiment of the erosion of definition."[39] Williams, however, not only blurs boundaries *within* the play; he also blurs the boundaries between audience and stage, and several times the audience is directly addressed and asked to participate in the illusion:

> *Felice.* (He comes forward and speaks pantingly to the audience.) The audience is supposed to imagine that the front of the house, where I am standing now, is shielded by sunflowers, too, but that was impractical as it would cut off the view.
>
> (5:353)

> *Felice.* Of course you realize that I'm trying to catch you and hold you with an opening monologue that has to be extended through sev-

eral—rather arbitrary—transitions, only related in a general way to—
(He gestures toward the statue with eyes shut tight).[40]

In terms of dramatic form, this direct acknowledgement of the audience exposes the play's self-consciousness as performance and the characters as performers.

This ultimate effect of Felice's speeches is, however, very different from the effect created by the employment of this device in the earlier works. Although one could argue that in *The Glass Menagerie* the audience is directly addressed as well, the situations have different intentions and effects. In *The Two-Character Play* Felice's speeches to the audience call attention to the fact that the play-within-a-play is a conscious construction, but this device also reminds the audience that every play—including, of course, the one they are watching at the present moment—is a carefully contrived and ordered representation of a particular way of perceiving reality, rather than a faithful reproduction of it. While in *Menagerie*, Tom's soliloquies to the audience make it clear that he, like Felice, is the author of his own play, these speeches don't interrupt the central narrative of the realistic "fourth-wall" drama. Rather, they serve the purpose of furthering the action of the story, of putting the audience in a position which makes it even more possible to participate in realistic identification and get lost in the illusion that they are watching a slice-of-life. His narration creates a similar effect as the images projected on a screen, the purpose of which was, as Williams pointed out in his production notes to the play, "to give accent to certain values in each scene." Williams felt that "the basic structure or narrative line may be obscured from the audience" (1:132), and his intention for Tom's monologues and the screen device was to emphasize and clarify the narrative core while simultaneously offering the audience a supplemental level of representation—the illuminating consciousness through which the "realistic" scenes are ultimately evaluated.

In a different manner, Big Daddy's monologues in *Cat on a Hot Tin Roof* also serve to strengthen the realistic goals of dramatic tension and identification rather than expose them as artificial constructions. When Big Daddy tells his infamous "elephant story" in act three of *Cat*'s Broadway version, for example, Williams has him cross to upstage center and "face front" to recite his tale in order to capture the audience's attention and increase their suspense as he involves them directly in the unfolding of his narrative:

> Big Daddy. [XUSC, face front.] This afternoon was a warm after-noon in spring an' that ole elephant had somethin' else on his mind which was bigger'n peanuts. You know the story, Brick?
>
> (3:205)

Moreover, since it was Kazan who persuaded Williams to add the revised third act, this speech is ultimately Kazan's contribution, and it reflects the "unrealistic" staging that he wanted for Big Daddy's monologues.[41] Given the play as a whole, however, the audience probably doesn't experience any break with realistic staging even when Big Daddy does come upstage center. In *Sweet Bird of Youth* as well, Williams makes use of a speech which di-rectly address the audience, although in this case the device pro-duces a somewhat different effect than either *Cat* or *Two-Character*. On the one hand, Chance Wayne's closing speech clearly fulfills a realistic purpose, since he ends the play by pleading with its members for their identification:

> Chance. [Rising and advancing to the forestage.] I don't ask for your pity, but just for your understanding—not even that—no. Just for your recognition of me in you, and the enemy, time, in us all.
>
> (4:124)

Yet there hasn't been any context in this fundamentally realistic play to prepare the audience for Chance's direct address, and so in another sense this final moment can also be seen as a break from realistic convention, and therefore as a transition from the primarily realistic appearance of this device in *Cat* to its strictly antirealistic employment in *Two-Character*.

In terms of content as well, Felice's speeches dismiss the illu-sions of realism, as Felice, like Tom in *Menagerie*, reveals an "author," the thought process of the creative mind behind the drama. Yet while both figures suggest an "author," Felice, unlike Tom, dissects the illusion of a finished product presented to us as an organized whole, as he comes forward and explains to the audience some of the choices and justifications behind the com-position of the play. Felice even anticipates the stage directions of the action through dialogue, explaining to the audience: "And now I touch her hand lightly, which is a signal that I am about to speak a new line in *The Two-Character Play*" (5:355). In *Menag-erie*, the audience accepts Tom as "the author" without eliminating Williams from its awareness as the "real" author of the entire presentation. In the case of Felice, however, the sense of instability—questioning the identity of the "real" author—is a central dimension of the play's complexity. Felice not only exposes *Two-Character* as his conscious construction, but the blurred distinction between the play's title and that of the play-within-a-play complicates the concept even further since the audience is not sure which play is "his" construction.

Williams' exposure of the instability of identity in terms of both "character" and "author" is yet another element in this work which blurs constructed boundaries and shatters illusions of wholeness. Felice is not exclusively a character in both the external and internal drama, he is simultaneously the author of the internal play, or at least is so according to the illusion of Williams' construction. Therefore, the play's metatheatrical element extends into an element of "meta-authorship." In "The Discourse on Language," Michel Foucault writes that it is the author "who implants, into the troublesome language of fiction, its unities, its coherence, its links with reality."[42] By playing with the stability of the concept of authorship, Williams is challenging the boundaries between text and author, as the author becomes just another role or character, and there is no single authoritative voice on which to rely. This is one more way in which meaning is made ambiguous in *The Two-Character Play*, as the truth or reality associated with locating meaning cannot be pinned down. Similarly, Felice is looking for a stable identity, a release from the burden of multiple roles. At the same time however, there is a fear of stability, of being "confined" (the "prohibited word") to one role and not being able to "Go back into the play" (5:366). At one point Felice suggests to Clare that he is growing his hair for the role of Felice. When she objects that "The part of Felice is not the only part that you play," he replies, "From now on, it might be" (5:320), a comment ambivalent with both desire and apprehension. Felice craves stability, yet simultaneously fears the limitations of being "confined" to one role.

Just as the boundaries between reality and illusion and the boundaries between author and text are blurred in this play, the boundaries between truth and lies are also thrown into question. Felice describes "truth" as "sick, sick—aberrations!" (5:315). One problem that he and Clare face in their search for truth is that the dialogue (which is all they've got) is shown not to have the power to represent any stable reality or central truth. They are trapped in the cycle of representation—in the dialogue—which they must repeat night after night. Felice cries out to Clare to "Stop repeating, repeating!" (5:327), and his outcry could be seen as a plea for release from the language and the theater that traps him. The characters are trapped in *The Two-Character Play* (both Williams' play and the play-within-a-play), from which there is no escape except for the silence of death or the confinement of the asylum, and both alternatives cause fear and panic.

One way of reading this play could see Clare and Felice as representing a debate, or meditation, between two voices within one mind, concerning the fear of confinement and the loss of control, both artistic control and the loss of emotional, mental, and linguistic control known as madness. Clare remarks that when Felice was locked away at State Haven, the mental institution, he "allowed [himself] to lose contact with all reality," as he had "Stopped speaking! Stared without recognition!" (5:346). Losing contact with language meant losing contact with reality. The words of the insane are suspect, and Foucault discusses how, historically, the words of the mad have been isolated, either rendered completely invalid or considered to utter a deep, mystical truth:

> From the depths of the Middle Ages, a man was mad if his speech could not be said to form part of the common discourse of men. His words were considered nul [*sic*] and void, without truth or significance. . . . And yet, in contrast to all others, his words were credited with strange powers, of revealing some hidden truth, of predicting the future, of revealing, in all their naivete, what the wise were unable to perceive . . . . [F]or centuries, in Europe, the words of a madman were either totally ignored or else were taken as words of truth. They either fell into a void—rejected the moment they were proffered—or else men deciphered in them a naive or cunning reason, rationality more rational than that of a rational man. At all events, whether excluded or secretly invested with reason, the madman's speech did not strictly exist.[43]

By throwing the sanity of Clare and Felice into question, Williams dislocates truth even further. Not only are boundaries between reality and fiction (play-within-a-play), author and text, and truth and lies disrupted in this work, but the very reliability of the characters and the words they speak in the text become suspect. We (as audience), however, are not *only* thrown into uncertainty concerning the issue of whether the characters are mad or sane. Even if the characters were represented as unequivocally insane, there still would exist the uncertainty of whether their words were "nul [sic] and void, without truth or significance," or whether they revealed "some hidden truth"—an uncertainty which undermines any sort of stable center we might try to impose upon this drama.

The play's central characters, Clare and Felice, have been said to represent Williams and his sister Rose, or, as some have argued, two sides of Williams himself. Dakin Williams believes that

> It is too easy to assume that the incestuous, or near-incestuous relationship stands for Tennessee's love for his sister. It is more likely that Felice and Clare are two facets of Tennessee himself, full of all the inner terror that did indeed haunt him at the time.[44]

Whether or not the two characters in this play stand for Williams and his sister Rose or two sides of Williams himself, it is clear that this is a very personal play. In 1973 Williams called it "a history of what I went through in the Sixties transmuted into the predicament of a brother and a sister."[45] The earliest versions of *The Two-Character Play* were written during Williams' very difficult period of depression, which began after Merlo's death in 1963 and was complicated by the fear and paranoia caused by various drugs and alcohol. Williams continued to revise this play after his forced three-month confinement for rehabilitation in Barnes Hospital in 1969, when the constant fear of insanity and the threat of confinement were to take on a central importance in his work. Leverich writes that "In one way or another, [Williams] was always in flight from confinement in all its guises, which he described as the greatest dread of his life."[46] The pervasive fear of being institutionalized for insanity had been present in Williams' mind throughout most of his adult life, especially after the confinement of his sister Rose as a young adult, but the realization of this fear in 1969 had further increased his terror of being committed. Elia Kazan has said that Williams "was absolutely terrified of confinement and of breakdown. And of course there was the example of Rose."[47] Rose's confinement in a private sanatorium in 1929 was the beginning of a series of confinements for mental and emotional troubles which led to the family's decision in 1943 to allow doctors to perform a lobotomy, rendering Rose incapable of an independent life.[48] In fact, up until her death in 1996, Rose was financially supported by Tennessee and lived in a private sanitarium. Even after his death, a statement in his will ensured that her care would always be paid for.[49] Williams' feelings of guilt (and, simultaneously, powerlessness) for not directly objecting to Rose's lobotomy, along with his own fear of the horrors of institutionalization, are undeniably present in the later work. His description of the sense of powerlessness and fear while trying to "survive" in the violent ward of Barnes Hospital in the face of insanity echoes the mood of his later plays:

> I dutifully came to their atrocious meals and the rest of the time I crouched like a defenseless animal in a corner while the awful pageantry of the days and nights went on, a continual performance of horror shows, inside and outside my skull.[50]

This "continual performance of horror shows, inside and outside [his] skull" is one he repeats over and over throughout his later period. Boxill feels that "*The Two-Character Play* (1967) becomes accessible when seen not as an attempt to tell a sad tale on stage so much as a theatrical exploration of psychic pain."[51]

Williams was feeling increasingly alienated from his audiences in the 1960s, as well as increasingly alienated from himself and his own writing. He was attempting to express his ideas and emotions in a new way to a new generation, yet felt trapped in his own language. In 1979 Williams articulated this awareness of being trapped in his desire to create and express, a desire which can only be effectively silenced through death: "I've been working like a son of a bitch since 1969 to make an artistic comeback, . . . there's no release short of death."[52] Hume Cronyn, the husband of Jessica Tandy, the original Blanche of *Streetcar*, read the script of *The Two-Character Play* early on, before the play was ever produced. After seeing the first staged production of the play in London in 1967, Cronyn described what he felt was Williams' "problem" during the 1960s:

> It's as though he were writing on a different plane, on a different level, and somehow the form and pressure of this time is escaping him and he is seeking desperately to find some way of expressing himself to the world of today, particularly to the young people of today. In *The Two-Character Play* that quality came over very, very strongly. I mean that terrible effort to reach out to say what had to be said. The whole setting, the dark theatre, the sense of being locked in, the quality of alienship, if there is such a word. There was only one person in the world with whom he had any kind of relationship at all, or either character had. And even that was half fantasy. If [sic] was a dream world in which somehow two people were baying at the moon.[53]

Williams' fear of being "locked in" is not only evident in the physical sense in this play ("confined," Clare and Felice repeatedly emphasize, is the "prohibited word"), but also in the sense of being trapped in his own creation. The sense of losing control of one's creation—losing a sense of boundary between author and text—is evident both here and in *Tokyo Hotel*. In 1960 Williams remarked that

> When the work of any kind of creative worker becomes tyrannically obsessive to the point of overshadowing his life, almost taking the place of it, he is in a hazardous situation. His situation is hazardous for the simple reason that the source, the fountainhead of his work, can only be his life.[54]

George Niesen points out that Williams "has indulged his penchant for creating in his plays characters who are artists of one sort or another. . . . The artist attempts to give some kind of meaning to life and death."[55]

The Two-Character Play, however, does not depend on Williams' autobiographical details and personal concerns for its significance; in a number of respects, it is a complex and sophisticated work which stands entirely on its own. In a 1979 interview with C. Robert Jennings, Williams said that *Out Cry* was his "most beautiful play since *Streetcar*," but that "the critics will say I am excessively personal and I pity myself."[56] This is what the critics often did say about *The Two-Character Play/Out Cry*, and about much of Williams' later work in general. These evaluations rest on a typical misreading of *The Two-Character Play*, a purely autobiographical one in which critics focus excessively on the personal aspects of the play and refuse to explore it on its own terms. Ronald Hayman, for example, sees the essence of *The Two-Character Play* as a therapeutic working out of Williams' confusion during the 1960s, and he posits that the play "can be read as an attempt to do for himself what neither of his psychoanalysts had been able to do for him. He was trying to recover the goodness, the purity he had lost, and he still tended to identify the loss with the loss of Rose."[57] Norman J. Fedder similarly claims that in *The Two-Character Play* "Williams is more determined than ever to 'confess all'—this time through the mouths of a sibling duo intent on performing their *Two-Character Play* of psychotic self-revelation."[58] Although this play does indeed stem from personal psychic pain, the charge of being too personal or too autobiographical is not valid in consideration of its ability to stand alone as a work of art. In fact, the most literally autobiographical play of Williams' career, *The Glass Menagerie*, succeeds not only because of its representation of characters and situations which the audience can recognize and identify with, but also because of its ability *to suggest effectively an interpretation of the experience of living in the world* to which the audience can relate. *The Two-Character Play* achieves the same end, although instead of arriving there by representing and exploring the conditions of external reality, it does this by going beyond externals—drawing attention to and deconstructing the paradoxes of living in and with the language that has constructed both our realities and ourselves.

When *Out Cry* opened in Chicago, William Leonard of the *Chicago Tribune* summed up the play by taking a phrase from the dialogue—"ponderously symbolic undrama."[59] Arthur Ganz was of the opinion that the characters in *Out Cry*, like those of the later plays in general, were "so recognizably close to Williams and his concerns, [that] the pity extended to them [was] ultimately self-pity, an emotion of very limited dramatic appeal."[60] When he called *Out Cry*, along with *In the Bar of a Tokyo Hotel* and *Small Craft Warnings*, "rambling discourses with little or no movement toward a climax,"[61] he was refusing to acknowledge that the more antirealistic drama that Williams was trying to create self-consciously avoided the "movement toward a climax" characteristic of realistic drama. Therefore, Ganz, like other critics, was judging Williams' later work on criteria which may have been appropriate to the earlier realistic plays, but was not compatible with the "new" theater he was working on from the 1960s until his death.

Many of the critics who have discussed *The Two-Character Play* have misread its essential nature, seeing it as an unsuccessful and unremarkable attempt at realism with some peripheral non-realistic elements thrown in. Ganz, for example, describes *Out Cry*, a version of *The Two-Character Play*, in realistic terms, claiming that it is a play

in which a brother and sister (suggestive of the figures in *The Glass Menagerie*), the leaders of a traveling acting company, find themselves immured alone in a mysterious foreign theater. There—on a stage dominated by a terrifying black statue, the symbol of their psychic torments—they act out a play about a brother and sister immured alone in a house dominated by ghosts of a past domestic tragedy. Unfortunately, the Pirandellesque element of the play within the play is handled without sufficient theatrical flair, and the obsessive concern with finding a private world sheltered from the assaults of external reality finally becomes stultifying.[62]

Ganz apparently sees the play-within-a-play element as the only one which distinguishes *Out Cry/The Two-Character Play* from realistic narrative drama, as he reduces it to a work "about" a brother and sister in a specific location and stable situation, assumptions which the drama constantly and effectively resists. What he posits as the characters' goal—their "obsessive concern with finding a private world sheltered from the assaults of external reality"—is more appropriate to Blanche in *A Streetcar Named Desire* than to the situation in this play. Ganz's comparison of *Out Cry* with *The Glass Menagerie* indicates both his focus on a superficial aspect of character (the brother-sister relationship), and his desire to understand the construction of character in the same way for both works. His inability or unwillingness to see *Out Cry* as a radical departure from the early Williams canon is typical of the kinds of criticism that positioned the later works as failed reproductions of his early plays and is apparently a central reason for Ganz's disappointment. Peggy W. Prenshaw has made a similar comparison between *Out Cry* and *Menagerie*, claiming that *Out Cry* "in some respects is like a sequel to *Glass Menagerie*."[63]

Niesen asserts that "With *The Two-Character Play* Williams has finally achieved a new intellectual statement," but he goes on to reduce the play's overdetermined web of meaning to a realistic commentary about the plight of the artist, claiming that "despite its dramatic failings," *The Two-Character Play* "is a *cri de coeur*, a plea for survival and for a place to be somebody, a play which . . . clearly delineates the problems the artist faces in trying to survive in a hostile environment."[64] Charles B. Brooks called the characters in *The Two-Character Play* "ridiculous," claiming that

> they unsuccessfully try to talk themselves into doing something to escape their plight. When the insurance company refused to pay on their father's policy on the 'legal technicality' that it was forfeited in case of suicide, they appealed in the interests of humanity, fully expecting to be taken seriously.[65]

Like Ganz and Niesen, Brooks is reading the play with realistic expectations, rather than with the ironic detachment it calls for. The majority of critics were judging Williams' later plays from a position which did not suit his work any longer; clearly, by the 1960s, a new set of conditions was needed to evaluate Williams' dramatic offerings.

The Two-Character Play provides an experience rich in linguistic play which emphasizes the instability of language and character and brings out the complexities of expression and presentation. It reacts against the constructed unities of realism, as realism's debt to the "well-made play" rests on its tendency to undermine any attempt at representing a particular character's sense of discontinuity, dislocation, or fragmentation as anything more than individual aberration from a fixed and stable "human nature." This play rethinks constructed notions of the real by challenging the linguistic boundaries that define truth, and it denaturalizes the relationship between truth and representation by calling attention to its own creation. Unlike realistic works, which present finished and seamless products that desire to conceal the history of their own making, *The Two-Character Play* self-consciously and deliberately exposes itself as construction, reminding the audience that the actor is not the character and the representation is not the thing represented.

At the core of this work is Williams' fundamental observation of the way in which human experience inevitably undermines the very limited rational structures and boundaries that language provides for its expression. Williams makes a sophisticated statement concerning artistic representation by exposing the complications and contradictions involved in the logical ordering of human action, thought, motivation, and desire—as well as by breaking down the hierarchy of truths on which realistic presentation depends. He presents his audience/reader with an irrational and overblown sense of fear which, rather than serving as the basis for a linear plot development which would attempt to *express* the human condition, permeates and dominates the atmosphere of the play as it *becomes* the human condition. The weariness of struggling to function emotionally and socially by trying to confine oneself to the demands of the frustrating prison of linguistic expression—with the dreaded alternatives of madness, confinement, silence, and death looming pervasively in the background—is the vehicle through which human existence and perseverance is explored. Leverich writes that

> While it has been argued that [Williams'] later work suffered from a conscious effort to create art, I believe that on close examination it can be shown that his struggle to fuse the poetic with the dramatic is as much in evidence in these so-called minor works as it was in his major plays. He was as much concerned as ever in his final efforts with the depths and origins of human feelings and motivations, the

difference being that he had gone into a deeper, more obscure realm, which of course put the poet in him to the fore, not the playwright with his concern for audience and critical reaction.[66]

With *The Two-Character Play* Williams finally achieves his desire to move away from the signifying speeches of realistic representation and toward a presentation of his artistic vision in a "more direct form . . . that fits people and societies going a bit mad."[67]

4

Weak Dramatic Experiments and the Reluctant Return to Realism

"I can't think of any area of the theater that I haven't tried to explore. I've written realistic plays, I have written fantasies, I've written allegories."
—Tennessee Williams, interview with John Gruen, 1965

THE FAILURE OF *CAMINO REAL* IN 1953 WAS VERY MUCH ON WIL-liams' mind when he set out to experiment with various conventions and dramatic modes after *The Night of the Iguana*. It was with the negative critical reception of *Camino Real*, Williams often said, that he began to feel he was losing his command over the theater. He had realized that this play "was a real departure from convention,"[1] but still had believed that it "most surely would be recognized for eloquence of language and certain passages." He was deeply insulted that the play "was simply dismissed by the critics, just laughed at," and was devastated to witness that audiences, too, were not impressed:

> I remember in Philadelphia I was very angry on opening night. Great blocks of people would get up and start walking out, and I would get in the aisle and try to turn them back into their seats. I'd scream and peg things at them.[2]

Since the negative reception of his plays would often plunge him into "an almost psychotic state of gloom,"[3] Williams wanted desperately to please the critical establishment as well as his audiences during the later period by giving them the more "conventional" realistic drama they were inclined to praise. At the same time, however, he was no longer interested in these traditional

110

forms, and he did have faith that his antirealistic experiments would eventually be recognized:

> I think the best thing you can do about the critics is never say a word. In the end you have the last say, and they know it. They can close your play, but if it has vitality it will be done again. Sooner or later they will accept it.[4]

Consequently, some of the plays that he wrote throughout the 1960s and 1970s, such as *The Milk Train Doesn't Stop Here Anymore* (1963, 1964) and *The Red Devil Battery Sign* (1975, 1979), are bizarre compromises—unconvincing and confused combinations of realism, melodramatic allegory, surrealism and several other experimental dramatic techniques. These plays, not surprisingly, failed with both critics and audiences.

By the late 1970s the failure of *Milk Train* and *Red Devil* had been augmented by the negative reception of Williams' more strictly antirealistic plays discussed in chapter three—especially *In the Bar of a Tokyo Hotel* and *The Two-Character Play*—and Williams' frustration with the critics led him to abandon periodically all departures from realism toward the end of his career. He attempted to return to the more strictly realistic kind of drama that had established his reputation in plays such as *Vieux Carré* (1977, 1979) and *A Lovely Sunday for Creve Coeur* (1978, 1980). Because of his persisting lack of commitment to realism at this time, however, these works often come across as weak attempts at realistic drama which lack the strong central action, effective poetic language, or complex characterization that were the trademarks of his earlier successes.

The Milk Train Doesn't Stop Here Anymore hails the beginning of Williams' later period, yet concerns itself with a familiar motif of the earlier work, one most obvious in plays such as *Orpheus Descending* (as well as its earlier version, *Battle of Angels*), for example, and *Sweet Bird of Youth:* the vagabond ("fugitive kind") male artist seeking shelter in the home of a lonely, emotionally hardened, and overtly sexual older woman. A realistic form constitutes the dominant dramatic style in *Milk Train:* the function of the dialogue, the specific setting representing "the library and bedroom of the white villa" (5:3), the formulation of a plot that depends on conflict, and characters meant to portray actual human beings dealing with life's struggles all follow the basic pattern of traditional realism. While this is undoubtedly a very personal play, it does not aim toward the representation of an internal psychology seen in some of Williams' more interesting anti-realistic later works, such as *I Can't Imagine Tomorrow, In the Bar of a Tokyo Hotel,* and *The Two-Character Play.* Instead, its realistic essence specifically indicates the exploration of characters in an interpersonal situation typical of the earlier plays.

Flora (Sissy) Goforth is, à la *Sweet Bird's* Alexandria del Lago, "a once beautiful but now aging ex-showgirl who makes it clear . . . that she is no longer filled with the milk of human kindness."[5] The play takes place during "the two final days of Mrs. Goforth's existence" (5:7), and she is writing her memoirs in her mountain top villa on Italy's Divina Costeira with her secretary, Francis Black ("Blackie"), as her only companion. Because of her wealth and "her reputation as a patron of arts and artists" (5:85), however, she is besieged by "free-loaders . . . writers that don't write, painters that don't paint" (5:19), and this particular summer Christopher Flanders makes his way up her mountain hoping to induce her patronage. Chris, a thirty-five-year-old traveling poet and mobile sculptor, has acquired the title of "angel of death" as a result of his reputation for bringing sexual and emotional companionship to rich, dying ladies on the Italian Riviera, and therefore Mrs. Goforth, not ready to leave this world just yet, is not all that willing to offer him her hospitality. But despite her initial resistance toward him, Mrs. Goforth desperately seeks Chris's companionship during her last moments before death, and finally offers him the food she had been denying him since his arrival the day before, along with "a long siesta together in the cool of my bedroom which is full of historical treasures, including myself!" (5:111). Chris, however, declines both offers. Instead, he sets out to comfort "an elderly spinster lady whose mother died in Taormina" (5:112), but not without helping Mrs. Goforth to her deathbed and easing the pain of her fear and loneliness with his companionship, promising to be there when she wakes up, which, of course, she never will.

In terms of its strictly realistic elements alone, *Milk Train* is far inferior to Williams' typical construction of complex characters and poetic style, as can be seen simply from the awkwardness of the title's rhythm, cadence, and imagery. A departure from many of his more compact and melodious titles, this one is a lengthy complete sentence which rhythmically falls dead and lacks any romantic associations. The awkwardness which begins with the title extends to the rest of the play: Hayman writes that "the characters are overexplained and the rhetoric is overblown."[6] Unlike the earlier plays with similar premises such as *Orpheus* and *Sweet Bird*, *Milk Train* fails to provide the elements necessary for effective realism. The plot is devoid of any significant conflict and the character development is weak. There is no actual emotional or sexual relationship between Mrs. Goforth and her "fugitive" artist. The plot is essentially concerned with Mrs. Goforth's suspicion of Chris's intentions, and his arrival on the scene merely serves as the interruption of her writing rather than as the occasion for the awakening of either genuine love or sexual gratification. Mrs. Goforth's character is explored only superficially, and although there is an attempt to provide a "history" for her through the recitation of her memoirs, what we do learn about her character is not particularly sympathetic or illuminating in the context of the play's action. Chris's character is hardly explored at all, and the ambiguity surrounding his past serves to confuse rather than entice. The audience gets no sense whatsoever of his true motivations, thoughts, or desires throughout the play, and his departure at the end sheds no further light on whether he is actually an ill-fated "angel of death" or simply a wandering poet who befriends rich old women as a means of financial survival.

Mrs. Goforth's secretary, Blackie, is not a very significant character in her own right and serves only as a foil to Mrs. Goforth's suspicious outlook and jaded disposition. Blackie's sympathy toward Chris seems to stem from her desire to rebel against Mrs. Goforth, who treats her with abusive disrespect. The only character of some interest in this play is "The Witch of Capri," a marchesa who "looks like a creature out of a sophisticated fairy tale, her costume something that might have been designed for Fata Morgana, . . . her expressive, claw-like hands . . . aglitter with gems" (5:42–43). Well-acquainted with the social scene on the Italian Riviera, The Witch visits Mrs. Goforth and relays the gossip concerning Chris and his experiences with dying old women. Throughout the play she is given some notable speeches and, although a minor character, manages to make an impression. Other than her expository function, however, The Witch is expendable to the plot, and it seems that Williams created her simply in order to have an interesting character in this play.

Milk Train has been described by Robert Bechtold Heilman as one of "the morality plays that are remarkably frequent in the modern theater."[7] Heilman claims that

> On the face of it, Sissy Goforth's struggle against death is rather like a melodramatic struggle against an omnipotent adversary raised to a

level of significance and dignity. . . . There is not the primary split that is at the center of *Everyman,* the archetypal play about dying. But Williams is writing for a different world.

In some ways this is a valid reading, and of course the allegorical name (charactonym) of Mrs. "Go forth" as a symbol of human endurance in the face of the fear and pain surrounding death is in line with this interpretation of *Milk Train* as containing elements of a modern morality play. Chris's character also takes on an allegorical function, yet one which is ambiguous: he is both the "angel of death" and the "savior" of his "patrons." The Christ symbolism demonstrated through Chris is not only evident in his allegorical function, but also, as Boxill reminds us, in the subtlety of his name (Chris/Christ) which, "like Val Xavier's, suggests salvation."[8]

One main reason for *Milk Train's* inadequacy is that in many ways it is an excessively personal play. Spoto believes that *Milk Train* was Williams' attempt "to come to terms with his relationship to Merlo, to articulate in death what was unspoken in life,"[9] and Mrs. Goforth, like Merlo in the midst of inoperable lung cancer, seems to be dying of "a chest abscess" (5:34). When Chris is on the phone trying to comfort a woman whose mother had just died, his final words are *"accept* it . . . *Accept* it" (5:94)— clearly Williams speaking to himself regarding Merlo's very recent death. The callous, irrational, and pathologically frightened Mrs. Goforth could be seen as an extension of Williams' fears of death, aging, and loneliness, and, like him, "She eats nothing but pills: around the clock" (5:30) in order to quell these fears. But unlike the meditations on fear that he was to write later on, in this play fear is not a pervasive dread which can't be located and is expressed only through truncated dialogue and awkward silences. Mrs. Goforth is able to articulate her fears through language in the manner of realistic drama: "Oh, God, Blackie, I'm *scared!* You know what I'm scared of? Possibly, maybe . . . dying this summer!" (5:13). But one of the reasons that this character fails in terms of realistic identification is that her fears are never explored, her character never understood on a level beyond the superficial. There is no identification with any of the characters in fact, and identification is necessary for the kind of realistic framework that *Milk Train* seeks as its support. Williams had often acknowledged that this play "reflected a great preoccupation with death."[10] But while he was able to stylize and express this preoccupation in effective dramatic forms with *I Can't Imagine Tomorrow, The Two-*

Character Play, and *In the Bar of a Tokyo Hotel,* he could not effectively dramatize his fears in *Milk Train.* The main problem with the personal element in *Milk Train* is not simply that it is excessive, but rather that this element is not developed in a way appropriate to the realistic dimension of the play. Because of *Milk Train's* dominant realistic structure, Williams could not find a way to produce one of the antirealistic meditations on fear and death that he was to write later on.

Although the dominant structure of *Milk Train* is essentially realistic, what qualifies this play as the first of Williams' later experiments is the fact that he added to its realistic dimension a number of devices that break sharply with realism, and which represented his new commitment to antirealistic forms. The most obvious of these is the allegorical dimension of the play. It is true that in the earlier plays Williams had often given his characters names which implied a symbolic significance, such as Valentine Xavier (both are saints' names), Chance Wayne (wane), and Alma ("Spanish for soul") Winemiller, but in these instances the effect was subtle and did not take on an overbearing significance. In *Milk Train,* however, the dominant charactonym is not subtle, as it is consciously stressed several times throughout the play: "Sissy Goforth's not ready to go forth yet and won't go forth til she's ready" (5:95). This forced emphasis on Mrs. Goforth's allegorical name takes away from the thread of realistic illusion that runs through the play, yet this device is not part of any nonrealistic dominating structure. Moreover, the earlier characters mentioned above were autonomous and complicated characters in the realistic sense, not simply allegorical symbols. Although the dominant realistic narrative of *Milk Train* sets up a situation which would require complex realistic characters, the character of Sissy Goforth is somewhere between realistic character and allegorical symbol. For the most part she functions as a symbol for human endurance.

Allegorical elements such as these are not entirely incompatible with realistic drama since the symbolism can effectively be incorporated into realism's presentation of the world. In a play such as *Orpheus Descending* (and *Battle of Angels*), for example, the abundant allegorical elements can certainly fit comfortably with the dominant realistic form in terms of plot, action, and character. However, in *Milk Train,* elements such as the blatancy of the charactonyms and the overbearing allegorical significance of the characters' roles beyond any autonomy they may have as realistic characters serve to undermine the play's realism.

In addition to the allegorical dimension, Williams injected several other nonrealistic elements into *Milk Train* that divert the audience's attention from the fourth-wall illusion. The play makes use of "a pair of stage assistants that function in a way that's between the Kabuki Theatre of Japan and the chorus of Greek theatre" (stage direction to *Milk Train*, 5:3). These stage assistants not only work as stage hands but "Now and then . . . have lines to speak, very short ones that serve as cues to the principal performers. . . . They should be regarded, therefore, as members of the cast. They sometimes take a balletic part in the action of the play" (5:3). Williams' reason (or what he calls his "excuse") for this device was that he believed "the play will come off better the further it is removed from conventional theater, since it's been rightly described as an allegory and as a 'sophisticated fairy tale'" (5:3). Other than the insertion of this device, however, *Milk Train* has no resemblance to Kabuki or Greek theater, and there does not seem to be a purpose for its intrusion into the main action other than to "remove the play from conventional theater."

The stage assistants open *Milk Train*, but their deliberately antirealistic speeches—introducing themselves to the audience and explaining the core of the action—is inconsistent with most of the rest of the play. Williams might have had *Menagerie* in mind when he incorporated this device, but in the earlier play the device of Tom as narrator was consistent with the play's realistic goals. In *Milk Train*, the stage assistants exist to undermine deliberately the realistic focus of the play, resulting in a confusing contradiction. Moreover, the stage assistants' sporadic insertions of poetic commentary are out of place in the context of the main action. For example, after explaining that they are invisible to the actors except when in costume, Mrs. Goforth appears on stage to begin the play "officially." As she does, the stage assistants proclaim together that their "hearts are invisible too" (5:8). We never hear of their "hearts" again, and this poetic insertion seems pointless for "characters" who are not really characters, but functional devices. Sometimes, however, the commentary of these assistants does add to the play's sense of drama. When Mrs. Goforth is contemplating "the meaning of life," for instance, the stage hands intervene with a brief dialogue whose rhythm foreshadows the staccato exchanges of the later works which focus on linguistic play:

One. Charade. Game.

Two. [Tossing a spangled ball to his partner.] Pastime.

One. [Tossing the ball back.] Flora's Folly.

Two. [tossing the ball back.] Accident of atoms.

One. [returning the ball.] Resulting from indiscriminate copulation.
(5:61)

Overall, however, there doesn't seem to be any logic or organization to their appearances or interjections.

Although the deviation from realism in *Milk Train* is peripheral, unlike the nondiegetic devices in earlier plays such *The Glass Menagerie* or *A Streetcar Named Desire*—which were employed as a way of emphasizing the central point of each scene or drawing a precise distinction between reality and fantasy—the nonrealistic devices in *Milk Train* are thrown in with no logical organization or sense of the overall dramatic purpose. As discussed in chapter three, it seems that initially Williams didn't have any clear view in mind of what he wanted his new "experimental" work to accomplish when he set out to break away from traditional realism after *The Night of the Iguana,* and he was therefore exploring various nonrealistic conventions.

The overall result of Williams' abundant use of nonrealistic devices is a hodgepodge of historical dramatic modes and conventions that don't come together effectively—morality play, allegory, modern realism, expressionism (in some of the stage assistants' exchanges), melodrama, Japanese Kabuki, Greek theater. While some of these elements are not mutually exclusive, their combinations in *Milk Train* often lead to stylistic contradictions. Hayman believes that

> The play loses more than it gains from such stylistic idiosyncrasies, which indicate a lack of confidence. Williams was afraid that his kind of play was going out of fashion. He told interviewers that after relying too heavily on words and naturalism, he felt envious of such younger writers as Harold Pinter and Edward Albee, who appeared to have more freedom. In *Milk Train* the stylization clashes with the rhetoric and the emotionality.[11]

Unlike his reactions to the negative criticism which *I Can't Imagine Tomorrow, The Two-Character Play* and *In the Bar of a Tokyo Hotel* were to receive, Williams tended to agree with the dominant criticism of *Milk Train.* He admitted in 1971 that the character of Christopher Flanders was weak and poorly defined:

> He really didn't have depth. I didn't understand him myself. That's finally why the play didn't work. I was very ill and depressed at the

time. I understood the old woman Goforth, but one can never know if Christopher is really a good man who comforts dying women, if he is sincerely devoted to them, and if he really wants to help them endure their agony. I wanted to make him deliberately ambiguous, but I think that I made him too ambiguous.[12]

Although Williams revised this play several times, the problems with structural inconsistencies and superficial characterizations were never fully resolved. He considered *Milk Train* "the most frustrating experience" that he had ever been through: "It was never a successful piece of work. I keep rewriting it all the time, but I've never gotten it right."[13]

After the failure of *Milk Train* and the repeated critical failure of the "freer forms" he wanted to experiment with in the later phase of his career, Williams was determined to give critics and audiences the more traditional dramatic structures that they demanded. He considered *The Red Devil Battery Sign* (1975) to be a "return to the conventional pattern but with a most volatile subject matter"—the collapse of American society.[14] However, like *The Milk Train Doesn't Stop Here Anymore*, *Red Devil* lacks the strong central action, convincing character structure, and consistent logic that realism demands. Hayman calls the rhetoric "dangerously inflated" and says that the characters and the plot "are too weak" to bear the burden of social significance.[15]

Although *Red Devil* does have some significant strengths, this play fails in ways that *Milk Train* does not. In 1974 Williams called *Red Devil* "a tragic love story with a great deal of music."[16] While the construction of character and evocation of mood are a bit more effective and certainly more promising than in *Milk Train*, the play consists of two rather vague plots which are arbitrarily connected through some unconvincing incidents, culminating in a bizarre scene which "seem[s] to explode from a dream" (8:376). *Red Devil* centers on two characters, a state senator's daughter whom Boxill describes as "a half-crazed, rebellious aristocrat (Woman Downtown) reminiscent of Carol Cutrere in *Orpheus Descending*,"[17] and a mariachi musician of "Spanish-Indian blood" named King Del Rey ("King") with "an air of authority" and a "hint of bravado" (8:291) who is dying of a brain tumor. The play's central plot involves the Woman Downtown's knowledge of illegal investments connected to the Red Devil Battery company. She is hiding out at the Yellow Rose Hotel in Dallas since she apparently has stolen documents which hint at the company's involvement in the assassination of President Kennedy and betray a net of corruption involving "secret investments" enigmatically tied to the Vietnam War (8:337). After a traumatic childhood with a politically unscrupulous father and his secret Apache mistress led her to a "private school for disturbed children" (8:335) the Woman Downtown (we never know her real name) was eventually sent to be raised by her godfather, a man named Judge Collister who, at the beginning of the play, has checked her into the hotel to be held under "complete anonymity" (8:286). Now an adult, she has reacted against the corruption of her past represented not only by her father but also by the husband she has just left, a crooked mogul of the Red Devil Battery corporation who is apparently threatening her life in order to retrieve the documents she has stolen. The logic of the plot is further complicated by the uncertainty as to whether the Woman Downtown is experiencing paranoid delusions or reacting to a very real threat.

The play's secondary plot concerns King's struggle in relinquishing the power and self-reliance that, for him, identifies him as a "man," since his illness has made it necessary for him to be the "invalid dependent" of his wife, Perla (8:315). Before his brain tumor left him a bit unsteady both mentally and physically, King and his daughter, "La Niña," were successfully touring with a mariachi band on their way to stardom. Now La Niña is practically estranged from her parents, living and performing in Chicago on her own, and sharing an apartment with a man who is married but otherwise genuinely devoted to her. The dimensions of this plot involve the dynamics within the family—disappointments, power struggles, and the desire coupled with the inability to communicate love. There are also suggestive references to an excessive emotional attachment between King and his daughter to the exclusion of his wife, but these suggestions aren't pursued. La Niña does come home with her lover for a short visit to try and mend her relationship with her parents. The confrontation between King and this man culminates in King's acceptance of him (since La Niña is pregnant with their child) and both a reaffirmation and a relinquishing of patriarchal power as King goes off with a revolver to "die like a King" (8:366).

The connecting thread between these two plots is, not surprisingly in a Williams play, sex—despite Williams' insistence that although he had "used sex . . . to hold an audience" in Red Devil, that is not where the emphasis lies.[18] King's resentment toward his wife has led him to an affair with the Woman Downtown, whom he visits at her hotel each night. The hotel is the focus of the overlap of the two plots—after the Woman Downtown checks in, the Yellow Rose soon serves as the convention headquarters for the Red Devil Battery Sign convention (presumably so that the company's spies can watch her), and it also happens to employ the mariachi band that used to perform with King. The two main characters had united after King "saved" the Woman Downtown from some suspicious men who were allegedly spying on her in the hotel cocktail lounge and escorted her to her room.

There are several moments of tenderness and often beautiful poetic conversations reminiscent of Williams' early works in the relationship between King and the Woman Downtown, and we are able to recognize a glimpse of Blanche DuBois here. Hayman calls the Woman Downtown "yet another reincarnation of the faded aristocratic belle,"[19] and several scenes in *Red Devil* clearly evoke Blanche's flirtatious exchanges with both Stanley and, especially, Mitch:

> *Blanche.* We are going to be very Bohemian . . . [She lights a candle stub and puts it in a bottle.] Je suis la Dame aux Camellias! Vous êtes—Armand! Understand French?
>
> *Mitch.* Naw. Naw, I—
>
> *Blanche.* Voulez-vous couchez avec moi ce soir? Vous ne comprenez pas? Ah, quelle dommage!—I mean it's a damned good thing. . . . I've found some liquor! . . .
>
> *Mitch.* [Heavily]. That's—good.
> [She enters the bedroom with the drinks and the candle.]
>
> *Blanche.* Sit down! Why don't you take off your coat and loosen your collar?
>
> *Mitch.* I better leave it on.
>
> *Blanche.* No. I want you to be comfortable.
>
> *Mitch.* I am ashamed of the way I perspire. My shirt is sticking to me.
>
> *Blanche.* Perspiration is healthy. If people didn't perspire they would die in five minutes. [She takes his coat from him.] This is a nice coat. What kind of material is it?
>
> (1:344–45)

Like Blanche, the Woman Downtown plays with King's "down to earth" nature throughout *Red Devil*, juxtaposing his ethnic, working class background with the aristocratic style which comes across in her manner of speech:

> *Woman Downtown.* [To King.] . . . Will you be my escort? An unescorted lady is not allowed at the bar.
>
> *King.* Si. Con mucho gusto. . . . Charlie, give the lady a drink.
>
> *Woman Downtown.* . . . Strong drinks aren't good in hot weather, overheat you internally. Even in a cool room, I'm conscious of heat outside. People bring it in the room with them like—little moons of perspiration under the armpits.
>
> *King.* [Embarrassed.] I took a shower and put on clean white shirt just before I come downtown, but the shirt's already stickin' to me. I ain't crowdin' you, am I?
>
> *Woman Downtown.* Oh no. Am I crowding you? I find it hard to keep a completely vertical position when so tired . . . [She is leaning against his shoulder; then she removes an atomizer from her evening bag.] This is a cooling little imported fragrance, Vol de Nuit, translates to Night Flight.
>
> (8:292)

In general, however, the flirtatious and romantic scenes between the characters are unconvincing and serve mostly as exposition, as occasions to relay the characters' past and present situations to the audience, and as a weak link between the two plots.

Hayman states that Williams wrote *The Red Devil Battery Sign* on the assumption that "he could establish a correspondence between his personal crisis and the political situation,"[20] and Spoto calls the play a "disjointed, unclear story of political terrorism and social enmity."[21] Williams himself considered *Red Devil* "a political play,"[22] and it includes several scattered references to politics and social issues which, unfortunately, have no immediate connection to any comprehensive dramatic plot or structure. For example, in the first scene "Charlie the Barman" and one of his overzealous customers engage in a brief exchange concerning the Vietnam War:

> *Drunk.* Any goddam kid won't register for draft is a traitor to—
>
> *Charlie.* Yestuhday, f'rinstance, Nation'l Guard tried to round up those kids that live in the Hollow, west a city, register 'em. I tell yuh they couldn't get near 'em, blown up two squad cars with bottles of nitro!
>
> *Drunk.* Savages in city. Oughta go in there with flame throwers, burn 'em outa their dug-outs like we done gooks in 'Nam.
>
> (8:289–90)

We don't hear of the War again except in brief and vague references from the Woman Downtown, and even then she mentions it in a completely different context. Similarly, social commentary is interspersed throughout the play with no sustaining line of action:

> *King.* Shots between gangs in the Hollow. . . . Oh, it's not—not—put in headlines but—is going on all the time and people don't dare admit—how far it has—gone, no, not yet, but soon it will blast too big for—city—denies.
>
> (8:362)

Williams rewrote *The Red Devil Battery Sign* twice after insignificantly short runs in Boston and London, and the final, published 1979 version of the play is the one I address here. In 1975, working on the first revision after *Red Devil* closed in Boston, Williams claimed that he had rewritten it with "a strong straight story line." He believed that the crucial connection between the two characters lay in the fact that they were both "doomed":

> He is doomed by a malignant growth on the brain, which is coming back after an operation. She is going to be faithful to her early heritage and testify before Congress in the McCarthy hearings. She has decoded documents in her possession which are seized when her godfather is murdered.[23]

Williams' claim that *Red Devil*'s emphasis on doom was enough to support "a strong straight story line" doesn't hold up in light of the fact that the sources of the characters' respective conditions are completely different—King's has to do with a physical "accident" (8:314) over which he had absolutely no control, whereas the Woman Downtown's situation is much more complicated and motivated by abstract social, political, and personal issues. The vague and confusing moments of disclosure that communicate the characters' situations are not enough to motivate and sustain the plot, which is incredible and melodramatic. Furthermore, there is an aura of madness and paranoia surrounding the Woman Downtown's character, which makes her claims of political persecution suspect and ultimately has the effect of minimizing the reliability of the play's political message (assuming that the audience could figure out what it was). At the same time, however, events happen (such as Judge Collister's being murdered and mysterious men trying violently to prevent the Woman Downtown from leaving the hotel) which seem to indicate that her "paranoid" fears and suspicions are in fact grounded in reality.

The point at which this play completely falls apart, however, is the last scene. The Woman Downtown tries to persuade King to abandon his suicidal intentions and come back to the hotel with her. King's mental state has been rapidly deteriorating, and at this point he begins to see visions of the mariachi musicians, who dance around him in a fantastic manner. Suddenly a mariachi "Drummer," who earlier in the play had apparently been planted by the Red Devil Battery company either to blackmail or to physically harm the Woman Downtown (this is never made clear), appears in pursuit of his mark. King fires at the Drummer (who is not a hallucination) and hits him, at which point the Woman Downtown screams and falls to the ground clinging to her lover.

The play then makes a very absurd shift, exploding into surrealism as "a fantastic group" of "outlaw" adolescents "seem to explode from a dream" and enter upon the scene (8:376). Unlike the mariachis, however, these characters are not visions but part of the play's action on the realistic level. Williams writes in the stage directions that at this point "The play stylistically makes its final break with realism. This break must be accomplished as if predetermined in the *mise en scene* [sic] from the beginning, as if naturally led up to, startlingly but credibly" (8:376). It is difficult to imagine, however, how even the most creative director could accomplish this. The adolescents form a "gang" from "the Hollow"—a neglected part of town where underprivileged kids congregate and dig caves in the rubble, "heaving rocks at each other, some nights, shots, explosions, soft drink bottles with nitro" (8:362). Their leader is "Wolf," a "boy-man with a sense of command and an intelligence that isn't morally nihilistic. His speech is almost like gutteral [sic] explosions of sound with gestures" (8:376–77). As Wolf approaches, his voice manages to "rouse the Woman Downtown from her crouched moaning position over King's dead body," and she goes off with him as his consort, "offer[ing] no resistance" since she "recognizes or senses something rightly appointed as her final fate" (8:377). Wolf grants the Woman Downtown a name, but one no less mysterious or concealing of her own identity—he extends his identity to her and calls her "Sister of Wolf." The scene dims out as she approaches King's body and "utters the lost but defiant outcry of the she-wolf" while the adolescents of the Hollow "all advance, eyes wide, looking out at us who have failed or betrayed them" (8:378). The effect of the play's collapse into surrealism is one of confusion and disappointment. Williams' commitment to anti-realistic modes is evident in this surrealistic gesture, but the ending of *Red Devil* is inappropriate and insufficient for such a complicated plot, which would require the logical closure of realism in order to be effective.

In many ways the ending of *Red Devil* resembles that of *A Streetcar Named Desire*, but whereas Blanche's "final fate" was carefully mapped out throughout the play, rendering her removal to a mental institution on the arm of a "gentlemanly" doctor logical and probably inevitable, in *Red Devil* the denizens of the Hollow and their leader, Wolf, come out of nowhere. Williams once said that the events of *Red Devil* move "towards an inevitable conclusion,"[24] but the ending is far from "inevitable." The Woman Downtown goes with Wolf willingly as the two establish an instant and bizarre connection, never alluded to or foreshadowed at any level in the text of the play, even though there are several loose references throughout to the poverty and violence of the Hollow. The integration of street hoods into the play's ending (making them the center of it, in fact) is apparently meant to lend a social dimension, but the gesture is too vague and incomprehensible in light of the rest of the plot. As far as dramatic style is concerned, the hallucinatory appearance of the hoods is part of the action of the play rather than strictly a representation of madness and desperation, as it was in both *Streetcar* and in various moments throughout *Red Devil* (such as King's dying visions).

Spoto reads *Red Devil* as "a treatment of Williams's drug-induced paranoia, which he believed was mirrored by a national paranoia."[25] A hint to the significance of the play's pervasive paranoia as well as its hallucinatory ending comes from the title. While Red Devil was (conveniently for Williams) the brand name of a popular battery that was being advertised with a flashing neon sign during the 1970s, "red devil" is also a popular slang term for secobarbital, a barbiturate with the brand name Seconal which Williams used liberally throughout his later years and up until his death. But this is not meant to be a play which directly dramatizes the paranoia, fear, and madness that Williams was experiencing in his drug-crazed mind. *The Red Devil Battery Sign* presents itself (at least for the most part) as a realistic portrait of American sociopolitical issues, and in that respect the play fails miserably. Whereas in *I Can't Imagine Tomorrow, The Two-Character Play*, and *In the Bar of a Tokyo Hotel* the fragmented structures and disjointed language were justified as a means of directly and nonrealistically representing madness, in *Red Devil* there is an attempt at the construction of a linear and realistic plot which moves toward an inconsistent conclusion, ultimately resulting in a structural mess. Despite the play's inconsistencies, however, Williams told an interviewer in 1975 that *Red Devil*, along with *Streetcar, Menagerie, Camino Real,* and *Cat,* was "one of [his] five best plays."[26]

Although Williams considered *The Red Devil Battery Sign* to be a return to a more conventional dramatic style, the inappropriate surrealism of the play's ending and the focus on volatile contemporary sociopolitical issues locates this play in a very different category from his earlier, more traditional realistic plays. As he approached the late 1970s, Williams, more eager than ever to enjoy critical favor once again, reverted back to a more strictly traditional style and reliable subject matter in *Vieux Carré* (1977, 1979) and *A Lovely Sunday for Creve Coeur* (1978, 1980). *Vieux Carré* contains no examples whatsoever of the type of nonrealistic elements which Williams employed in *Milk Train* and *Red Devil* as a way of breaking away from realistic convention, and which characterized the essence of *I Can't Imagine Tomorrow, In the Bar of a Tokyo Hotel,* and *The Two-Character Play. Vieux Carré* presents a slice-of-life portrait of the tenants of a rooming house in New Orleans during the period between winter 1938 and spring 1939. For this play Williams turned to an earlier place and time, seeking to recreate his more bohemian days in New Orleans during the 1930s, and in the stage directions he gives the precise address of the rooming house—722 Toulouse Street in the French Quarter— which had been his actual residence during the period in which the play takes place. The central character/narrator is called "The Writer," whom Williams readily admits is a representation of himself "those many years ago" (introductory notes to *Vieux Carré*, 8:4), even though he told James Grauerholz in a 1977 interview that

> in my new play there is a boy who is living in a house that I lived in, and undergoing some of the experiences that I underwent as a young writer. But his personality is totally different from mine. He talks quite differently from the way that I talk, so I say that the play is not autobiographical. And yet the events in the house did actually take place.[27]

Although the address at which this rooming house once stood is now the site of a converted two-story building, at the time Williams lived there he occupied the attic floor of a three-story house, and he specifies this too in the stage directions. Clearly *Vieux Carré* is Williams' attempt toward the end of his career to return to an earlier and more dependable theme, style, mood, and location (New Orleans, the old South) in the hopes of recapturing the success of those initial years.

Vieux Carré is an episodic play with a tone of desperation which brings together a young wanderer (the Writer), a tubercular painter who initiates the young writer into homosexual experience (Nightingale), two pathetic old ladies (Miss Carrie and Mary Maude) who try to maintain illusions of gentility despite the fact that they have been reduced to picking their food out of the garbage, a black servant (Nursie) who struggles to keep her job even though she should have retired long ago, and an unlikely pair of lovers—Jane Sparks, a woman of genteel background from upstate New York who, although fatally struck with tuberculosis, now shares a room with a sleazy strip show barker named Tye McCool. Jane's ladylike manner and her sense of dislocation in her present environment is clearly reminiscent of Mrs. Hardwicke-Moore in Williams' poignant one-act play *The Lady of Larkspur Lotion* (1945, 1953), and two other characters in *Vieux Carré*, the rooming house's landlady, Mrs. Wire, and "the Writer," are only slightly altered versions of the same characters in the earlier one-act play.

Critically, this play was not successful. Walter Kerr called *Vieux Carré* "a 'memory' play in the style of 'Glass Menagerie,'" but regretted that *Vieux Carré* lacked the dramatic energy and coherent structure of the earlier play.[28] Similarly, Spoto has called this play "a series of free-associations, drawn on a poeticized past," and feels that "Scene images tumble haphazardly in *Vieux Carré*."[29] He sees its only value as "what it reveals about the mood and temperament of the playwright at the time of writing"[30] and claims that the characters simply "incarnate aspects of Williams."[31]

Vieux Carré, however, *can* stand alone as a work of art without an emphasis on autobiography; it resists the assumption of a linear plot which works through dramatic tension. It is a play of observation—a series of external character sketches tied together by virtue of atmosphere. Spoto's observations especially ignore the subtleties of Williams' play, offering superficial observation in place of insight. Although the characters in *Vieux Carré* are not grandiose in the tradition of Blanche DuBois or Amanda Wingfield, this can be explained by the fact that they are constructed from an external point of view—that of "the Writer"—rather than from the complex position of psychological understanding that characterized many of Williams' earlier dramas. To call the play "a series of free associations" is insensitive to what *Vieux Carré* tries to accomplish, since there is a form to this play which is intentionally not dependent on plot, but rather on mood.

This full-length play is an expansion of Williams' short story "The Angel in the Alcove" (1943, pub. 1948), which takes place in the same boardinghouse in New Orleans. Therefore, not only did Williams revert to his more traditional style in this play; he turned to a piece of writing which he produced during and in the mode of his earlier period. This short piece focuses on a young writer (Williams) recounting the story of a fellow tenant— the pathetic artist who reappears in *Vieux Carré*—who tries to deny to himself and to others that he is dying of tuberculosis, only to be suddenly and cruelly evicted by the landlady and told that "A case like you is a public nuisance and danger."[32] The young writer who witnesses this realizes that after the heartless incident with the young painter the comforting ghostly figure resembling his maternal grandmother whom he had seen nightly by the window of his room no longer comes to grant him sleep, and he takes this as a sign to move on from his residence.

Williams called "The Angel in the Alcove" a "story of mood . . . mostly mood and nostalgia,"[33] and the mood and atmosphere of romantic squalor, loneliness, and temporality in the representation of the fringe element of society gathering together in a shabby New Orleans boardinghouse form precisely the foundation of *Vieux Carré*. This emphasis on mood rather than plot exhibits yet another reversion to Williams' earlier days, as it is also the typical characteristic of one-act plays contemporary with "The Angel in the Alcove," such as *The Lady of Larkspur Lotion*, whose characters (as mentioned earlier) formed the basis for characters such as Jane, Mrs. Wire, and the Writer in *Vieux Carré*. While Williams claims that at first he thought it might be "a big mistake" to transfer this story to the stage lest the result be "insubstantial," *Vieux Carré's* evocation of mood is powerful enough to carry the play.[34] Boxill writes that "Such unity as this kaleidoscopic drama enjoys is primarily owing to its sense of place,"[35] and in his opening stage directions Williams calls for "a poetic evocation of all the cheap rooming houses of the world" (8:4). Much of the mood in *Vieux Carré* is generated by the poignant poetic language, and a central trademark of Williams' plays—characters who maintain a shred of nobility in the midst of degrading and pathetic conditions—is very powerfully represented in this play.

One of the most strictly realistic plays of Williams' later period, *A Lovely Sunday for Creve Coeur* (which even follows the three unities of action, time, and place), was the play he believed would put him back in favor with the critics and mark the return to his central place in the American theater. Like *Vieux Carré*, *Lovely Sunday* is set in the 1930s and marks a nostalgic return to the style, mood, and setting of Williams' early work. The play takes place in an "efficiency apartment" reminiscent of the St. Louis tenements of *Glass Menagerie:*

> It is in the West End of St. Louis. Attempts to give the apartment brightness and cheer have gone brilliantly and disastrously wrong, and this wrongness is emphasized by the fiercely yellow glare of light through the oversize windows which look out upon vistas of surrounding apartment buildings, vistas that suggest the paintings of Ben Shahn: the dried-blood horror of lower middle-class American urban neighborhoods. (8:119)

The central character of *Lovely Sunday* is Dorothea ("Dotty") Gallaway, who is presented as yet another recurrence of the woman with a "Southern belle complex" (8:186) looking for romance and security in a world which ultimately disappoints her. This time she appears as a "marginally youthful but attractive" (8:119) schoolteacher from Memphis living in a bleak St. Louis apartment during the Great Depression. *Lovely Sunday* deals (once again) with the theme of "going on"—of surviving in the face of life's struggles. The main action of the play involves Dorothea's anticipation of a proposal of marriage from the high school principal (Ralph Ellis) with whom she has had an affair. She waits all morning for "a very important phone call" (8:175) which she believes will bring this proposal, but the audience has already learned that a published announcement in the paper has revealed that he is engaged to marry someone else of a higher social status. Dorothea's roommate, Bodey—a frumpy, middle-aged woman of German descent who is hard-of-hearing—tries to protect Dorothea from this devastating news by tearing the announcement out of the paper and throwing it in the wastebasket. Meanwhile, Dorothea's colleague at Blewett High School, Helena Brookmire— "A stylishly dressed woman with the eyes of a predatory bird" (8:136)—drops by the apartment. Helena wants Dorothea to move into an expensive apartment with her in the fashionable end of town, where she plans on giving all-women bridge parties twice a week with "a nicely uniformed maid to serve" (8:185).

She has learned of the news concerning Ralph Ellis' impending marriage and believes that Dorothea should know the truth, "since the news will be all over Blewett High School tomorrow" (8:171). Eventually, Helena hints that she saw Ralph's name in the paper, which prompts Dorothea to search for the proper section and find it crumpled in the wastebasket, whereupon she learns the truth.

Like Blanche, Dorothea is left with no secure future after a hoped-for marriage is no longer a possibility. However, while in *Streetcar* Stella—deciding to believe what she must in order to "go on living with Stanley" (1:405)—sacrifices Blanche's chance for emotional survival by committing her to an asylum, Dorothea is left with a viable option after she is abandoned, even though it involves an unattractive life of drab domesticity with Bodey's practical, sincere, but decidedly awkward and unromantic twin brother Buddy—a man for whom she has no desire or interest since she insists that "My life must include romance. Without romance in my life, I could no more live than I could without breath" (8:133). Fearful of losing the people closest to her, Bodey encourages the marriage of Buddy and Dorothea in order to keep them both in her life. The other two woman in the play, Helena and Dorothea's neighbor, Sophie Gluck, symbolize her alternate and equally unappealing options: the decidedly unsatisfying companionship of Helena in an expensive apartment which she can barely afford, or the loneliness and eventual mental breakdown represented through Sophie, an unstable woman who is barely able to function on her own. Sophie is another woman of German descent who, left alone after the recent death of her mother, is afraid to go back to her own apartment, believing it to be "spooked" (8:162). She therefore intrudes constantly on Bodey and Dorothea, "sobbing and rolling her eyes like a religieuse in a state of sorrowful vision" (8:154) and babbling alternately in English and German. Remaining without a man is not an alternative for Dorothea since she believes that "I've got to find a partner in life, or my life will have no meaning" (8:133), and so the play ends with Dorothea going off to meet Bodey and Buddy for a picnic at Creve Coeur ("heartbreak") park in order to consider the option of a union with him.

There are several similarities between the situations and characterizations of Dorothea and Blanche DuBois: both are high school teachers, both are "Southern belle" types whose lives depend on an expected marriage, both hold an excessively romantic view of life and love, and both are disappointed in the end. Helena tells Bodey that

> Dorothea has always impressed me as an emotionally fragile type of person who might collapse, just suddenly collapse, when confronted with the disappointing facts of a situation about which she'd allowed herself to have—romantic illusions. (8:146)

The similarities, however, are superficial. Dorothea lacks the depth of character and internal struggle of will and morality that Blanche embodied so well. Dorothea is not a very "dramatic" character: she evokes no great amount of pity nor understanding from the audience, and her attempt at poignancy through the story of a failed love affair in her youth is a weak shadow of Blanche's tragic reminiscence of her young, poetic husband's suicide after she cruelly announced her discovery of his homosexual affair and mocked his tormented sexual identity. Boxill argues that, like Blanche DuBois and Alma Winemiller, Dorothea, "having invalidated in the past the sexuality of the man she idealized, is punished in the present by the man to whom she succumbs."[36] However, Dorothea's situation is very different from these earlier protagonists, precisely because she did not exactly reject and "invalidate" the sexuality of her lover. While Dorothea's story at the beginning of scene two revealing her doomed union with a young and talented musician could have been effective, it ends with the realization that the love affair could not be consummated because of his "chronic case of—premature ejaculation" (8:169), a condition which, however tragic in its own minor way, is no dramatic match for repressed homosexuality and violent suicide.

Superficial characterization, mediocre plot substance, and undistinguished language are the main reasons why this play does not stand out as a major accomplishment. Rather than expressing the poetic nuances of *Menagerie* and *Streetcar*, the language of the play includes childish puns—as in Bodey's excitement over the fact that the German butcher is consistently sympathetic to her need for examining her purchases: "Mr. Butts always lets me feel his meat" (8:122)—and the play's attempt at humor through a scatological exchange concerning Sophie's attack of diarrhea (8:163–64) is weak and distasteful.

A Lovely Sunday for Creve Coeur attempts the complex construction of realistic characters and narrative plot of Williams' early plays, but winds up presenting us with uninteresting fragments of former characters with an adequate, but undistinguished, plot.

The play's evocation of mood is not significant enough to supplement and rescue the plot, and *Lovely Sunday* presents no valuable insights into the world of the characters. Dorothea, Bodey, Helena, and Miss Gluck are not memorable or impressive characters, and Williams does not construct the conflict necessary for any dramatic tension in this play. Although *Lovely Sunday* is a decent example of the realistic play, it lacks a significant evocation of mood as well as the creation of powerful and outstanding characters.

Spoto calls *A Lovely Sunday for Creve Coeur* a portrait of "four emotionally unfulfilled women, each terrified of being abandoned" and argues that it is "another page in Williams's personal album, for the four driven, lonely women each speak from a part of the author's life" during the 1920s and 1930s.[37] The connection with Williams' personal past that Spoto stresses is, however, only superficial, and not very significant for an overall criticism of the play. He focuses on references to "the days of [Williams'] attendance at the Ben Blewett school and University High, the days at International Shoe, the front porch in Memphis, and the final acceptance of life's compromises."[38] The Blewett school is only mentioned in the play as the school where Dorothea teaches civics, and the International Shoe Company is referred to several times as Bodey's employer for the last twenty years. Williams' use of place names he had come across in his life doesn't justify calling the play specifically "personal," and *Lovely Sunday* is no more personal than any of Williams' other plays. For that matter, it is certainly no more personal than the work of any writer. As for the "final acceptance of life's compromises," this could hardly be said to be specific to Williams' life. Spoto's criticism doesn't address the central reasons why *Lovely Sunday* is an unimpressive work. The play is no more "a page in Williams's personal album" than any of his early successful plays; certainly *The Glass Menagerie* and *A Streetcar Named Desire* were driven by Williams' personal concerns. Undoubtedly Williams was able to identify with his most memorable female characters such as Blanche DuBois, Alma Winemiller, and "Maggie the Cat." In 1973 he asserted that these characters were indeed a part of himself: "I draw every character out of my very multiple split personality. My heroines always express the climate of my interior world at the time in which those characters were created."[39]

In a 1972 essay entitled "Too Personal?" which was intended for a preopening piece in the *New York Times* but became the introduction to *Small Craft Warnings* (New Directions, 1972) after the *Times* chose to interview him instead, Williams answered the charge of being "too personal":

> Is it or is it not right or wrong for a playwright to put his persona into his work?
>   My answer is: "What else can he do?"—I mean the very root-necessity of all creative work is to express those things most involved in one's particular experience. Otherwise, is the work, however well executed, not a manufactured, a synthetic thing?[40]

He goes on:

> So far I have spoken only in defense of the personal kind of writing. Now I assure you that I know it can be overdone. It is the responsibility of the writer to put his experience as a being into work that refines it and elevates it and that makes of it an essence that a wide audience can somehow manage to feel in themselves: "This is true."[41]

While Williams is acknowledging that all creative writing is inevitably personal in some way, the manner in which the personal is represented is one aspect that differs between his essentially realistic and antirealistic dramas. *I Can't Imagine Tomorrow, The Two-Character Play*, and *In the Bar of a Tokyo Hotel* are indeed very personal plays, but they are in no way "too" personal since they make the personal universal by suggesting a shared experience of living in the world. *A Lovely Sunday for Creve Coeur*, on the other hand, can only be seen as personal by those, like Spoto, who know too much about Williams' personal past. Similarly, a play like *Vieux Carré* does not depend on an audience knowing the personal aspects it represents, but these aspects can be an added boon for those members of the popular audience who vaguely know something about Williams' life. In the case of *The Milk Train Doesn't Stop Here Anymore*, the excessively personal nature of the play is indeed part of the problem, but only in the sense that Williams had not yet found a way of dramatizing his personal vision effectively in nonrealistic forms, as he finally did in *Can't Imagine, Tokyo Hotel*, and *Two-Character*.

The critical establishment's claim that much of Williams' later work failed because it was simply "too personal" masks the real reason why these plays were not well received: they were not entertaining enough in terms of the expectations that go along with the "sensitive realism" typical of Williams' earlier Broadway successes. And, as discussed above, *A Lovely Sunday for Creve Coeur* fails essentially because it is a weak version of a dramatic style which Williams was no longer committed to. Neither critics nor reviewers ever complained that *The Glass Menagerie* or *A Streetcar Named Desire* were "too personal," and no one complained about this quality in the last of Williams' plays to be staged during his lifetime—*Something Cloudy, Something Clear* (1981)—an interesting journey through Williams' past creatively staged in the atmosphere of a dream. The title itself refers to the alternating perception of his life at the time, reflected by the actual physical perception he experienced due to a cataract which had developed on one of his eyes. Despite its overtly autobiographical nature, this play managed to please most audiences and critics.

Williams' nostalgic return to the days before his success as a playwright is most evident in this work, "a memory play in the vein of *Menagerie* and *Vieux Carré*,"[42] whose central characters are based on Williams himself and on a young Canadian dancer named Kip Kiernan (also called "Kip" in the play) whom Williams knew in Provincetown during the summer of 1940. After a brief homosexual experience with Williams, Kip hurt and surprised him by marrying a young woman, and several years later he died of a brain tumor in his twenties. Williams has called *Something Cloudy, Something Clear* "one of the most personal plays I've written," and this blatantly autobiographical work evokes not only Kip but also Frank Merlo and Tallulah Bankhead, whom Williams met in Provincetown.[43] Boxill writes that in this play

> the Williams character appeared as a thirty-year-old writer in khaki trousers and unbuttoned shirt (August) who, while revising a play in Provincetown over the summer of 1940, meets a needy young man and woman, both fatally ill (Kip and Clare), with whom he plans to live later on in the autumn. All that actually happens is that he completes his revisions and initiates Kip into homosexuality.[44]

This play, however, is not a return to realism in the manner of *Vieux Carré* and *A Lovely Sunday for Creve Coeur*. The atmosphere of this play is often dreamlike and merges the events of Williams' past with a self-conscious present perspective, giving the central character the ability to explore his situation from several vantage points. Although Spoto claims that all who saw the play "loved it,"[45] the very heavy autobiographical foundation even to the point of undisguised characters, the fact that "voices from [Williams'] past and his future seem to address him from the sky,"[46] and the bizarre final dance of the characters at the end to Ravel's funereal "Pavane" make it difficult to make sense of this play apart from its significance as a poignant and therapeutic exercise for the playwright and a revealing sketch for those who are interested in his personal past. This play is one case, probably the only one, in which the charge of "too personal" can be justly leveled.

None of the plays discussed in this chapter were as artistically successful as Williams' earlier plays in terms of complex characterization, powerful dramatic conflict, and lyrical descriptive speeches, and none of them were as sophisticated as the later plays discussed in chapter three in terms of the direct exploration of the ways in which language constructs and manipulates our perceptions of reality. But while *The Milk Train Doesn't Stop Here Anymore* was a structural mess with little merit, *The Red Devil Battery Sign* did have the potential for effective characterization and plot, and *A Lovely Sunday for Creve Coeur* is a respectable, although mediocre, example of the realistic play. Of all the marginal later plays, however, *Vieux Carré* recalls Williams sentimental genius most effectively in its exploration of characters on the fringes of respectable society who separate themselves from the status quo and live anonymous lives of freedom with loneliness as its price. Williams' brand of loneliness in the best of his plays is the kind of romanticized human isolation that exists ironically in the midst of urban overcrowding. In *Vieux Carré*, Williams gathers together all of his pathetically noble examples of "the fugitive kind" under one roof successfully to create a touching atmosphere of human suffering, loneliness, and endurance.

Although the argument that Williams was *unable* to effectively write realistic plays during his later period as a result of his abusive relationship to drugs and alcohol *may* have some legitimacy, this argument assumes that Williams was still interested in writing realistically, and does not account for the fact that he desperately wanted to move away from his earlier style—a desire which the evidence clearly and repeatedly emphasizes. It seems more likely that the central reason why his later attempts at writing either predominantly or strictly realistic plays fail artistically is that he was forcing himself to conform to the critics' expectations against his own passionate interests. Williams' experiences with a critical establishment which could not shed their expectations of him as a realistic writer—and therefore brutally dismissed his antirealistic experiments during the 1960s and beyond—devastated him, and he wanted very much to be back in their favor.

5

Critical Expectations and Assumptions: Williams' Later Reputation and the American Reception of the Avant-Garde

"The job of the theatre critic is first of all to determine what the human significance of a particular play or performance is. In doing this he evaluates it. Every play or performance has a certain quality or 'weight' of life in it. The critic must try to define its essence and place it in some personal or traditional scale of values which the reader in his turn is permitted to judge."

—Harold Clurman, introduction to *Lies Like Truth*

"There is actually a common link between the two schools, French and American, but characteristically the motor impulse of the French school is intellectual and philosophic while that of the American is more of an emotional and romantic nature. What is this common link? In my opinion it is most simply definable as a sense, an intuition, of an underlying dread-fulness in modern experience."

—Tennessee Williams, introduction to Carson McCullers' *Reflections in a Golden Eye*

IN A 1975 INTERVIEW WITH CHARLES RUAS, WILLIAMS DENIED ANY allegiance with other playwrights or other schools of thought in drama, insisting that the "different" forms of his later period were entirely his own:

I'm quite through with the kind of play that established my early and popular reputation. I am doing a different thing, which is altogether my own, not influenced at all by other playwrights at home or abroad, or by other schools of theatre. My thing is what it always was, to express my world and experience of it in whatever form seems suitable to the material.[1]

135

Although Williams claimed that his later style was unique, he did often hail Samuel Beckett along with Harold Pinter and Edward Albee as major playwrights whose work he greatly admired,[2] and several critics have pointed out interesting parallels between Beckett's work especially and Williams' experimental plays. Therefore, since these playwrights were doing work similar to what Williams was doing in the second half of his career, it is certainly worthwhile to explore how they were received, both by the reviewers and by the critics, in order to illuminate further the extent to which Williams' reputation may be a product not of what he actually achieved but of the assumptions and biases of those who evaluated his plays.

Those evaluating Williams' later plays have often discussed them in Beckettian terms. James Coakley saw Williams exhibiting what has become known as a Beckettian view of the world as early as *Camino Real*, which was first performed in New York within a few months after *Waiting for Godot* was presented in Paris. Although *Godot* appeared in book form in 1952 (in French), it premiered in Paris in January 1953, and *Camino Real* had its first performance in March of that year.[3] Coakley, writing in 1977, argued that the "central perception" of *Camino Real* is that "life is no more than 'dim, communal comfort' eroded by change; values are illusory, perpetually in transit. How, in short, is one to live?"—a perception which he claimed is characterized by "a despair worthy of Beckett, priding itself upon no more than the black honesty of its vision."[4]

In *The Two-Character Play*, most obviously, Williams was aiming for a more Beckettian kind of drama, one that deliberately challenges orthodox notions of expression and meaning. George Niesen asserts that "The Beckettian echoes in *The Two-Character Play* are striking,"[5] and goes on to catalogue similarities between Williams' play and several of Beckett's works, including *Endgame* and *Waiting for Godot:*

> The set itself, the freezing, dimming "state theatre of a state unknown" (p. 313), the "prison, this last theatre" (p. 364), with its solitary slit of a hole in the backstage wall, is right out of *Endgame*. Felice's description of his own play, "It's possible for a play to have no ending in the usual sense of an ending, in order to make a point about nothing really ending" (p. 360), and his statement, "With no place to return to, we have to go on" (p. 316) apply equally to *Waiting for Godot*.[6]

Similarly, C. W. E. Bigsby draws attention to the parallels between *Out Cry* (*The Two-Character Play*) and the plays of Beckett, Pinter, and Albee, pointing out that

> movement is reduced to a minimum—physical stasis standing as an image of constraint, as a denial of clear causality and as an assertion that the real drama operates in the mind (which reinvents the past, translates experience into meaning and imposes its own grid on experience, denying death and acting out its own necessary myth of immortality). . . . The incompletions of the set underline the deconstructive thrust of the play which is a drama of entropy in which character, plot and language slowly disintegrate.[7]

Like Beckett's works, Williams' plays discussed in chapter three—*I Can't Imagine Tomorrow, In the Bar of a Tokyo Hotel,* and *The Two-Character Play*—defy realistic expectations of character, plot, action, and language in an attempt to raise central questions about the nature of reality and the role that language plays in its representation. In the same vein as plays such as *Waiting for Godot* and *Endgame,* Williams' later work focuses on the concept that language is the medium through which reality is constructed and defined rather than directly expressed. The typical situation presented in these plays involves characters who are trying to escape from a language which is neither an accurate nor a satisfying expression of their thoughts and desires. Yet the realization that language, however flawed, is the only means of conceiving their realities and themselves, traps them in the endless need to continue speaking. Therefore, a simultaneous frustration with and dependence on dialogue creates the "tension" in both Beckett's and Williams' plays, which experiment with the paradox of linguistic existence. While the purpose of discourse in realistic drama is typically the attempt directly to communicate truth or convey rational meaning, in the type of experimental drama discussed above discourse serves primarily as a diversion from the silence that would signal the annihilation of the characters.

In Beckett's works, communication often occurs through means other than language. In *Molloy,* for example, a work which takes the unreliability of language to an extreme, Molloy communicates with his mother by knocking on her skull.[8] In *Waiting For Godot,* dialogue, rather than being a vehicle for communication, is consciously used to occupy Gogo and Didi while they wait and divert their attention from the alternative—the silent void that signifies death. They often opt for language over action, telling stories to pass the time[9] rather than hanging themselves, even though the later activity would promise them the physical pleasure of sexual erection.[10] In *Endgame*, Nagg and Nell communicate with each other by knocking on their trash bins and rattling the cans. It is linguistic play, rather than the attempt directly to communicate meaning through language, which drives the action in Beckett's works. Clov asks Hamm, "What is there to keep me here?" and Hamm replies, "The dialogue."[11] Michael Vanden Heuvel points out that "Play, Beckett suggests, ultimately functions as a 'just' refusal of powerlessness and chaos because, despite its painful exertions, it remains a source of momentum."[12]

Similarly, for Williams, it is precisely the dialogue of *The Two-Character Play*—both Williams' play and the play-within-a-play in which the characters perform—that saves them from the silence they both desire and dread and enables them to "go on":

> *Clare.* [Overlapping.] Stop here, we can't go on!
>
> *Felice.* [Overlapping.] Go on!
>
> *Clare.* [Overlapping.] Line!

                                                                    (5:345)

Clare and Felice realize that although language is an inaccurate, unreliable, and essentially arbitrary construct in its relation to truth and meaning, it is all they have to define and affirm their existence. At the end of the play, when they are feeling trapped and it seems as though there's "nothing to be done" (5:366), Felice suggests that they "Go back into the play" (5:366), that is, the play-within-the-play. Like Beckett's characters, it is the only way for them to go on. In *Endgame*, Clov expresses his dissatisfaction with existing linguistic structures, telling Hamm "I use the words you taught me. If they don't mean anything any more [*sic*], teach me others. Or let me be silent."[13] The present language is not useful anymore as far as expressing truth is concerned, but the silence is worse. Even though there is "nothing to say,"[14] Hamm pleads with Clov to "Say something"[15] before he goes. Similarly, in *The Unnamable* the voice states, "Unfortunately I am afraid, as always, of going on,"[16] yet the fear of silence is even greater than the fear of continuing: "I shall never be silent. Never."[17] Therefore the impulse is finally "I can't go on, I'll go on."[18]

Despite the striking dramaturgical parallels between Beckett's work and many of Williams' later plays, both reviewers and critics reacted very differently to the two playwrights. Overall, the reception of Beckett's plays in the United States was much warmer than that of Williams' similar experimental dramas, which were of course never fully accepted by either reviewers or critics. Although American reviewers initially resisted Beckett's unconventional style, they eventually applauded his art as valid and original. The critics hailed Beckett's work from the beginning as mature, avant-garde, and philosophically engaging.

In 1957 a composer living in Chicago, Warren Lee, used the example of Beckett's reception in the United States to address what he saw as the cultural biases evident in the American critical reaction to theater and to literature in general which does not "divert and amuse." Although he uses the term "critics," Lee is unequivocally referring to the group I've designated as "reviewers." He insisted that his article, "The Bitter Pill of Samuel Beckett," written for the *Chicago Review*, was intended "less as a defense of Beckett (which isn't needed) than as an exposition of what he is saying."[19] Lee believed that

> A discussion of [Beckett's] "bitter pill" and the reasons for taking it will suggest critical standards that are sorely needed in this country. With a long-standing reputation for inhospitality to the best in contemporary literature, the Wealthy Man runs the risk of spinning idly in the shallows while the main currents of European thought pass by.[20]

Lee associates the "Wealthy Man" with the American public, and puts forth the notion that

> The Wealthy Man, who has no fear, will usually choose a literature that diverts and amuses. His closest association with meaning will be in writing that agrees with him and tells him what a fine fellow he is. Thus, for instance, *The King and I* and *The Moon is Blue* each enjoyed longer runs on Broadway than all of O'Neill's plays together.[21]

By contrast, Lee argues,

> The Anxious Man, on the other hand—the man who has fear, or at least doubt—will often prefer meaning and interpretation to diversion and ornamentation. (Not always, to be sure—but at least often enough to warrant the distinction). He also selects books that agree with him and that corroborate his values, but in a broader sense of the word, corroborate. And he may even undertake to hear the opposition once in a while.[22]

Lee associates the "Anxious Man" with a more European sensibility and understanding of literature. While it is not entirely clear what signifies "meaning" for Lee, he proposes that "It is the first premise of this essay that the primary value of literature is 'meaning'—*then* ornament."[23]

Lee's article is essentially a complaint about the commodification of theatrical and literary criticism in the United States and the unwillingness of the comfortable American "Wealthy Man" to accept a kind of literature—and specifically drama—which is not easily accessible and pleasantly entertaining, and which does not reinforce positive American cultural myths and values. Lee calls criticism an "essential commodity" in this country and believes that criticism, when "functioning properly, should bridge the gap between author and audience—discerning good literature, and expounding it when necessary." He argues, however, that in the categories of tragedy and tragicomedy, American critics "have accomplished a succession of impressive failures—failing on one hand to perceive fine writing, and then being unable to account for it after it has arrived." His argument is obviously applicable to the reviewers' reactions to the work of Williams and Beckett, and Lee does specifically mention both these authors. He hails *Camino Real* along with *The Iceman Cometh* as examples of the "fine writing" that American reviewers and critics failed to perceive, and argues for the superiority of the original—albeit more pessimistic—version of act 3 in *Cat on a Hot Tin Roof*, as he tries to illustrate some reasons for these errors in critical judgement:

> Many reasons come to mind. First, we are the Wealthy Man, isolated and safe. We can ignore certain melancholy truths—and even exert pressure to make sure they won't be brought up by authors: cf., the difference between *Camino Real* and *Cat on a Hot Tin Roof*—and, worse, the inferior version of Act III of the later, which Williams was persuaded to use.[24]

Lee goes on to discuss (with disdain) the "bafflement" of the American press when *Waiting for Godot* reached the States in 1956:

> Recently an important writer appeared in the person of Samuel Beckett, an Irishman writing in French; and the event proved to be a perfect occasion for American critics to demonstrate their theoretical limitations. Lacking proper equipment, most of those who acknowledged Beckett's appearance sounded like so many versions of Wolcott Gibbs, saying "Somehow the meaning of the piece eluded me." In

general they were baffled (and offended)—particularly by Beckett's play, *Waiting for Godot*.[25]

Lee's contention that members of the American critical establishment are "theoretically limited" and that they (as well as American audiences) seek "diversion and amusement" in theater and literature in general, is one which often proved to be true in the case of Williams' later work as well as some of his less "sensitive" and "benign" earlier plays. Once we slide from theater/literature to film, the American critical bias for the safe, the morally right, and the pleasant becomes blatantly obvious. We only have to witness how Hollywood altered the endings of both *The Glass Menagerie* and *A Streetcar Named Desire*—ensuring that its audiences would be subjected to as little unpleasantness as possible—in order to conclude what American criticism values in its art/entertainment (in Hollywood, the distinction is already blurred). The atrocious conclusion of the film version of *Menagerie* showed Laura happily adjusted to society—fortified rather than destroyed as a result of the experience with Jim—and excitedly awaiting the arrival of a new gentleman caller who presumably will be the answer to her (and Amanda's) prayers. The film version's altered ending of *Streetcar*, while more subtle, was still clearly an effort to force the conclusion to correspond with American morality. Of course, especially in the case of *Streetcar*, and especially during the 1950s, Hollywood was also contending with the Roman Catholic Legion of Decency and was forced to consider its influence where sexual or other "inappropriate" film content was concerned. Williams' sexually suggestive film *Baby Doll* (1956), for example, was condemned by both the Legion of Decency and Francis Cardinal Spellman as "immoral," generating a great deal of controversy. Both the Motion Picture Code and the New York State Board of Censors, however, ultimately approved the film for release after Elia Kazan agreed to a number a excisions. While Williams' ending of *Streetcar* has Stella sobbing "luxuriously" and "with inhuman abandon" in Stanley's arms as he "voluptuously, soothingly" comforts her, kneeling beside her while "his fingers find the opening of her blouse" (1:419), at the end of the Hollywood version Stella directly reacts to the brutality Stanley has shown throughout the film—his striking of her on the poker night, for example, and his cruelty to Blanche. She sweeps her baby into her arms, tells Stanley to never touch her again, and goes up to Eunice's house for protection from this brute of a man. He is justly punished for his evil, Stella exhibits strength, morality, and independence, and the audience is satisfied. Never mind that in the play the fact that Stella stays with Stanley despite all that has come between them is a central aspect of the power that lies in the sensuality of their relationship. The play's ambivalence concerning whether she is acting out of weakness or strength, and whether she is right or wrong to stay with him, adds to the complexity and effectiveness of the ending, but the moral implications of these issues were too dangerous and controversial for the standard Hollywood mentality.

In *Lies Like Truth*, Harold Clurman wrote of the tendency of reviewers to avoid addressing the connection between the disturbing issues that are brought to light in American drama (he specifically mentions Williams and Beckett) and the recognition of these issues in American culture at large. The American tendency, he argues, is to dismiss the distressing "pessimism" of certain plays as "incomprehensible" in order to avoid confronting it in our own culture:

> We do not say that we cannot abide the pessimism in *Camino Real* (it is not pessimistic but romantic); we say it is incomprehensible. We do not confront the core of *Godot*'s bitterness; we say it is unintelligible. We do not object to the brutality in Shakespeare because we do not actually relate to Shakespeare: he represents "poetry"—which may be translated as high-minded entertainment.
>
> The tendency then is to retreat from the essence of every serious play even when we applaud it, so that we may think of it simply as an amusement. Thus, though we may prize *A Streetcar Named Desire* as an absorbing show, we generally avoid saying what it signifies to the American scene.[26]

The reviewers' rejection of disturbing aspects of Williams' early work which Clurman brings out and, I would argue, of the more pessimistic message and unconventional style of his later work, was rooted in the fundamental expectations of an established theater criticism which reflected American political values and assumptions of the 1950s and early 1960s.

The reviewers who established Williams' early reputation but regarded his later work with disdain were divided in their reactions toward *Waiting for Godot* when it hit New York in 1956. While the group as a whole essentially admitted that the "intellectualism" of the play was beyond their ken, some reviewers were, as Eric Bentley puts it, "respectful towards what was not fully understood," while others, like Walter Kerr for example, found "something of a scandal in the very existence of difficulty."[27] Kenneth Tynan described the response of the New York press to *Godot* as "baffled, but mostly appreciative," and informed his readers that the play's reception was prefigured by "an advertising campaign in which the management appealed for 70,000 intellectuals to make its venture pay."[28] Beckett's reputation as an "intellectual" was established primarily through his association with Joyce and the avant-garde. In 1957 A. J. Leventhal wrote of Joyce's influence on Beckett in *The Listener*, but he asserted that "Beckett is in a sense a more intellectual writer than Joyce and his jousting with words has a background of erudition deeper, one suspects, than that of the Master—the *cher maître* of the *avant garde* of the 'twenties and 'thirties in Montparnasse."[29]

Walter Kerr, like several of his colleagues, seemed to take offense at what he saw as Beckett's pretentious intellectualism and insensitivity to "what goes on in the minds and hearts of the folks out front," and wished that Beckett were more "in touch with the texture of things." He wrote in the *New York Herald Tribune* that "*Waiting for Godot* is not a real carrot; it is a patiently painted, painstakingly formed plastic job for the intellectual fruitbowl."[30] John Chapman complained in the *Daily News* that "Thinking is a simple, elementary process. *Godot* is merely a stunt," and in the *Daily Mirror* Robert Coleman wrote that "The author was once secretary to that master of obfuscation, James Joyce. Beckett appears to have absorbed some of his employer's ability to make the simple complex."[31] In London, W. A. Darlington called *Waiting for Godot* "a queer play which nobody pretends to understand very clearly."[32]

The more "respectful" press, while praising the philosophical seriousness of the play and the artistic validity of the writer, were nonetheless inclined to point out that *Waiting for Godot* was a puzzling piece, and certainly not for all tastes. In a 1956 review for the *New York Times*, Brooks Atkinson called *Godot* "a mystery wrapped in an enigma," but went on to praise it as "an allegory written in a modern tone" that incorporates symbolism which, although elusive, "is not a pose." Beckett's drama, he decides, "adumbrates—rather than expresses—an attitude towards man's experience on earth." From the beginning of his review, Atkinson brings up Beckett's association with Joyce, and he looks to Beckett's French and Irish predecessors for an interpretation of his message, claiming that Beckett's "acrid cartoon of the story of mankind" is forged through a combination of Sartre's "bleak, dark, disgusted" point of view, and Joyce's "pungent and fabulous" style. Atkinson's piece abounds with bewilderment and even dislike concerning the drama itself, remedied by praise for the sheer physicality of the acting. Although he calls *Godot* an "uneventful, maundering, loquacious drama," he hails Bert Lahr in the role of Gogo as an actor "in the pantomime tradition who has a thousand ways to move and a hundred ways to grimace in order to make the story interesting and theatrical, and touching too." Overall, Atkinson concludes that Beckett is a "valid writer," and that although *Godot* is a "'puzzlement' . . . Mr. Beckett is no charlatan. . . . Theatregoers can rail at it, but they cannot ignore it."[33]

Audiences, however, did not always agree. Kenneth Tynan points out that when *Godot* was performed in London in 1955, "many of the first-night audience found it pretentious."[34] When the play reached the United States, the first Miami audiences were "bitterly disappointed" after the enormous build-up the play received from abroad, and walked out of the theater in disgust.[35] By the time the play reached Broadway some months later, however, New York audiences were generally appreciative, but, like Atkinson, were largely responding to Bert Lahr's "noble performance."[36]

Atkinson's reaction to Beckett's second play, *Endgame*, was similar. He starts off his 1958 review by crediting the director and the actors with the play's artistic success.[37] Lewis Funke's 1962 review of the same play proclaims that "whatever else may be said of Beckett, of his personal attitudes toward life, of his lack of hope, no one can deny that he possesses an artist's witchcraft. He is able to weave spells in the theatre." Like Atkinson, Funke believed that "The Theatre of the Absurd is not for the general taste. Nor, however, can it be denied."[38]

These reviewers reacted to Beckett's avant-garde contemporaries—such as Harold Pinter—in much the same way, but there was less controversy overall concerning the acceptance of Pinter's work since Beckett had paved the way for the "Theatre of the Absurd" in Britain and the United States. In *Thirty Plays Hath November*, Walter Kerr writes that "Every playwright whose work is genuinely original goes through a trial period of resistance and doubt, followed by a time of advancing rumor. On his first exposure to Broadway, with *The Caretaker*, Pinter had been banished after a short run."[39] Just as with Beckett's introduction to New York, however, there were champions of Pinter's Broadway debut. In 1961 Harold Taubman wrote in the *New York Times* that

Out of a scabrous derelict and two mentally unbalanced brothers Harold Pinter has woven a play of strangely compelling beauty and passion. "The Caretaker," which opened last night at the Lyceum, proclaims its young English author as one of the important playwrights of our day. . . . A work of rare originality, "The Caretaker" will tease and cling to the mind. No matter what happens in the months to come, it will lend luster to this Broadway season.[40]

British reviewers were often also ambivalent about Pinter's works overall—in a review of *The Homecoming* in 1965, B. A. Young wrote that "London's critics . . . were generally disappointed by the play"[41]—but he was eventually accepted in Britain and the United States to the point where even Walter Kerr considered himself a "dedicated Pinterite."[42]

Clearly the reviewers had expectations and prescribed standards for judging drama which blatantly affected their evaluation of both the unconventional plays of Beckett (and the other dramatists) which were becoming popular in the late 1950s, and Williams' similar later plays. After an initial period of outrage, however, reviewers were willing to give Beckett and Pinter the benefit of the doubt when faced with plays which baffled their conventional expectations, while the same courtesy was never given to Williams. Factors such as Beckett's overwhelming success abroad, his association with Joyce and with the established tradition of French existentialism, and finally pressure from the intellectual community at large led to an acceptance of and eventually enthusiasm for Beckett and those playwrights who followed him. Atkinson wrote in 1958 that "Although it is impossible to construct a story or theme out of 'Endgame,' after the manner of realistic drama, Mr. Beckett's point of view is adumbrated in the dialogue. Life is meaningless, he says."[43] Furthermore, Atkinson's comparisons of Beckett's dramas with the work of Joyce and Sartre—and later with "a Picasso abstraction"[44]—are typical of the associations that aided in building Beckett's reputation as a serious artist. When Williams, however, "adumbrated" the same point of view through his dialogue, the reviewers stopped at "baffled" and concluded that Williams was either drugged, burnt-out as a writer, or unsuccessfully trying to imitate Beckett.

The critics' reactions to the work of Beckett and Pinter were from the beginning clearly more enthusiastic and admiring than that of the reviewers. Like the reviewers, they often referred to Beckett's intellectual background, specifically his association with Joyce. John Gassner called *Waiting for Godot* "Beckett's Joycean masterpiece,"[45] and praised the philosophy behind Beckett's repetitious and minimalistic language:

> In drama of the absurd, language has once more been undercut by moody repetitions that make progression of feeling and thought impossible; this is apparent even in such well-written plays by Samuel Beckett as *Krapp's Last Tape, Endgame,* and *Happy Days.* In some of these, words, which have been the carriers of ideas in the theatre ever since Aeschylus, have even been subordinated to mechanical sounds and movements as a preferable means of communication.[46]

Gassner decided that both Beckett and Pinter were writing plays which "provided a concentration of mature feeling with worthy skill and control that set them apart from other new plays as products of a virtually different world of theatre than the customary commercial product." He applauded the *New Yorker's* description of *Happy Days* and *Waiting for Godot* as "mysterious, frightening, funny and altogether remarkable."[47]

Eric Bentley believed that *Waiting for Godot* was an "important play," yet he felt that while Beckett's voice was "interesting," it was "not quite . . . individual" nor "new" since "Mr. Beckett is excessively—if quite inevitably—overinfluenced by Joyce." Bentley insisted that "one is tempted to think that Irish literature, even when it is written in French, as Beckett's play was, is cut from those coats of many colors, *Ulysses* and *Finnegan's Wake* [sic]."[48] Overall, however, Bentley defended Beckett's dramaturgy, and called *Godot* "a landmark":

> *Waiting for Godot* seems antidramatic in that garrulity is the all-but-declared principle of its dialogue. These men talk to kill time, talk for talking's sake. It is the opposite of *azione parlata,* which implies "a minimum of words, because something important is going on." Here we seem to have a maximum of words because nothing at all is going on—except waiting.
>
> But this is a big exception, and it saves Beckett's play. it makes no difference that the waiting may be for nothing. Here is a play with a very slight Action, with only the slightest movement from beginning to middle to end, and yet there *is* an Action, and it enables us to see the totality, not as *un*dramatic, but as a parody of the dramatic.[49]

In *The Theatre of Revolt*, Robert Brustein called Beckett "the most gifted" of the theatre of the absurd dramatists,[50] and in 1956 Kenneth Rexroth wrote in *The Nation* that

> Beckett is so significant . . . because he has said the final word to date in the long indictment of industrial and commercial civilization

which began with Blake, Sade, Hölderlin, Baudelaire, and has continued to our day with Lawrence, Céline, Miller, and whose most forthright recent voices have been Artaud and Jean Genet.[51]

When Kenneth Tynan reviewed *Godot* at its London debut, he asserted that "It forced [him] to reexamine the rules which have hitherto governed the drama; and, having done so, to pronounce them not elastic enough. It is validly new."[52] Like the other critics, Tynan enthusiastically explored and defended Beckett's dramaturgy and his philosophy:

By all the known criteria, Samuel Beckett's *Waiting For Godot* is a dramatic vacuum. Pity the critic who seeks a chink in its armour, for it is all chink. It has no plot, no climax, no *dénouement*; no beginning, no middle, and no end. Unavoidably, it has a situation, and it might be accused of having suspense, since it deals with the impatience of two tramps, waiting beneath a tree for a cryptic Mr. Godot to keep his appointment with them; but the situation is never developed, and a glance at the programme shows that Mr. Godot is not going to arrive. *Waiting for Godot* frankly jettisons everything by which we recognize theatre. It arrives at the custom-house, as it were, with no luggage, no passport, and nothing to declare; yet it gets through as might a pilgrim from Mars.[53]

The critics more closely allied with the academic community were similarly writing in praise of Beckett's philosophical position and his dramaturgical style. As early as 1955 Edith Kern wrote in *Yale French Studies* that "It is Beckett's genius to have found the simple word, the absurdly comical situation to express his thoughts on man's place in the universe."[54] She asserts that "by all traditional standards *Waiting for Godot* is not a play" since "It has no action and thus completely lacks what Aristotle considered the most essential element of a successful play," there is "no character development" and no "plot or any kind of suspense." In spite of this she believes that "author and director manage to convey to the spectator a sensation of high drama, of a tragic fatality wedded to laughter which hides behind the exuberance of slapstick."[55] Kern concludes her article with the grand evaluation that

Beckett's characters in this play glorify . . . the all-surpassing power of human tenderness which alone makes bearable man's long and ultimately futile wait for a redeemer and which, in fact, turns out itself to be the redeemer of man in his forlornness.[56]

The critics' evaluations of Pinter were, like those of the reviewers, similar to their evaluations of Beckett. Gassner writes that *The Caretaker*

> is a haunting work as well as an exciting one; even the humor is wry and enigmatic. . . . *The Caretaker*, regardless of my minor dissatisfactions with the work, coheres for me magically and makes sense as a poetic (though not necessarily "anagogical") realization of a "feeling" about humanity. It is possible, I would conclude, to derive gratifications from Pinter's play on both literal and imaginative, or *reflective*, levels.[57]

Arthur Ganz praised Pinter as well, claiming that he "has known as much as any modern playwright the appeal of the liberated self. He has sensed, and embodied in the plays, that impulse toward the unlimited expansion of the ego, toward dominance, luxury, action, possession, sensual gratification." Ganz even went so far as to align Pinter with "the first great modern playwright," Henrik Ibsen, on the basis that they share "a kind of grim humor . . . [and] an essentially ambiguous view of the human condition," despite their very different styles.[58]

While the work of avant-garde playwrights such as Beckett and Pinter was praised by the critics as innovative, intelligent, and philosophical, Williams' similar experiments were, of course, dismissed by them as failures most of the time. The critics were hailing dramaturgical qualities in Beckett's work that were clearly present in Williams' later plays, but they were not willing to grant Williams the intellectual capabilities that would enable him to produce a serious work of art in the tradition of the avant-garde. Precisely the same qualities that the critics praised in Beckett and Pinter's work, they condemned and complained about in Williams' later plays. Gassner's contention that in Beckett's plays, as well as in other works in the tradition of drama of the absurd, "language has once more been undercut by moody repetitions that make progression of thought and feeling impossible" could just as easily be applied to Williams' *I Can't Imagine Tomorrow, In the Bar of a Tokyo Hotel*, and *The Two-Character Play*.[59] Apparently for Gassner, Williams was more a part of the "customary commercial product" which, unlike the plays of Beckett and Pinter, did *not* provide "a concentration of mature feeling with worthy skill and control."[60] Similarly, Bentley's description of Beckett's dramaturgy in *Waiting for Godot* as "a parody of the dramatic,"[61] and Tynan's praise for *Godot* as an artistic success which "gets through" despite the fact that it is a "dramatic vacuum" which "frankly jettisons everything by which we recognize theatre," are qualities which many later plays of Williams exhibit.[62] In Williams' case, however, his dramaturgy was not recognized as a deliberate attempt to undermine traditional convention; rather, he was criticized for failing to uphold those very conventions "by which we recognize theatre"—or at least the essentially realistic, commercial theater for which Williams was known.

Overall, it was Beckett's reputation as an "intellectual" from the beginning of his career which anticipated the critics' reactions to his work and helped establish him within the elite circle of serious avant-garde writers which also welcomed Pinter and Albee. Williams, on the other hand, was excluded from this elite circle primarily on the basis of his early reputation. The critics were never prepared to take Williams seriously. From the beginning of his career they looked upon him as the pop hero of Broadway, and they were not about to budge from that position long enough to form a careful evaluation of his later work. This attitude is clearly illustrated in an anecdote concerning John Simon, who is generally known for his vicious attacks on playwrights and performers rather than for overly praiseful criticism. When Simon—who went on to become the drama critic for *New York* magazine—was a student at Harvard University, he wrote a rave review of *A Streetcar Named Desire* for the *Harvard Advocate*. The editorial board "thought he must be crazy for his enthusiasm" and consequently he lost his job.[63] While at times the critics did recognize the power and originality of the plays which were in general spurned by the reviewers, they still maintained their own assumptions and set of prescribed standards concerning Williams' work. They had serious reservations concerning the artistic validity of a playwright who was so well established on Broadway and in the popular American cinema, and therefore were often inclined to casually dismiss Williams' later plays as either pretentious and empty philosophical ramblings or weak and superficial imitations of Beckett's style.

The overall consensus of the critics during the second half of Williams' career was (similar to the reviewers) that either he was so exhausted from his indulgences with drugs and alcohol that he was unable to think coherently, or that in his twilight years he must be running out of ideas for new plays and was therefore desperately and pathetically trying to imitate the popular avant-garde drama of his younger contemporaries. Even some of Williams' personal acquaintances felt this way. Spoto writes that when Williams was working on *The Two-Character Play,* his friends saw his new offering as "a strange dialogue for two characters that suggested . . . an imitation of Pirandello or Pinter."[64] And when Vassilis Voglis, an artist who knew Williams socially for several years, claimed that Williams "turned to Beckett's *Godot* for his *Two-Character Play* and to other plays by other writers later" after "he lost contact with his roots,"[65] the implication is, once again, that Williams was no longer able to write originally and so was engaging in simple imitation of the newer successful artists. These remarks are emblematic of the critics' attitude toward his later work, an attitude which combines scorn with pity. Essentially, the response from Williams' friends and acquaintances to resemblances between his later work and the new drama contemporary with it was the assumption that Williams must be getting desperate, since he couldn't possibly be "intellectual" enough to turn his hand at "serious" drama.

In his later years, Williams was defeated before he ever began; reviewers tended to exhibit hostility toward experimental drama in general, and Williams never had a chance to be taken seriously in the first place by the critics. His later reputation, therefore, tells us more about the critical biases in the popular and academic press in this country than about Williams' work per se. In most critical texts on theater and drama, Williams is hailed as one of America's greatest playwrights, but he is referred to as if he died after *The Night of the Iguana*. The later plays are mentioned only in passing, if at all, and then usually with either brutal disdain or pity for the loss of talent in the great artist who, by the 1970s, was perceived as having been reduced to a babbling, drugged-out, dirty old man—capable of expressing himself only through the lewd ramblings of his *Memoirs*.

Notes

Preface

1. Albert J. Devlin, ed., *Conversations with Tennessee Williams* (Jackson: University Press of Mississippi, 1986), 318.
2. Bruce Smith, *Costly Performances: Tennessee Williams: The Last Stage* (New York: Paragon House, 1990), 30.
3. Dotson Rader, *Tennessee: Cry of the Heart* (New York: Doubleday, 1985), 193–94.
4. Donald Spoto, *The Kindness of Strangers: The Life of Tennessee Williams* (New York: Ballantine Books, 1985), 321. Even though I use Spoto's 1985 biography of Williams, primarily in chapters 1 and 4, to present a general impression of the atmosphere surrounding Williams' later reception and point out some typical attitudes and observations concerning Williams' reputation, this edition should be viewed with caution for any serious study of Williams' career. It is riddled with inaccuracies, which I point out when necessary, and in chapter 4 I often take issue with Spoto's critical observations of Williams' work that rest on false premises. Lyle Leverich's 1995 biography of Williams, *Tom: The Unknown Tennessee Williams* (New York: Crown Publishers), is a much more accurate scholarly project and certainly supersedes Spoto's work. Leverich, however, only deals with Williams' life up to his success with *The Glass Menagerie* in 1945, and I am mostly concerned with the years after this, which is why I use Spoto in conjunction with Leverich. For the same reason, I sometimes refer to Ronald Hayman's 1993 biography, *Everyone Else Is an Audience* (New Haven: Yale University Press), which is overall a much more accurate study than Spoto's, although still not as thorough as Leverich's. Leverich was Williams' chosen biographer, and the scheduled publication date for his second volume of Williams' life is January 1999.
5. Elia Kazan, *Elia Kazan: A Life* (New York: Doubleday, 1988), 495.
6. Tennessee Williams, in a taped interview with Stephen Banker in the *Tapes for Readers* series, 1974, quoted in Spoto, *Kindness of Strangers*, 291.
7. Louis Auchincloss, "Tennessee Williams: The Last Puritan," *Dictionary of Literary Biography: Documentary Series* 4 (Detroit: Gale Research, 1984), 410. Quoted in Spoto, *Kindness of Strangers*, 322.
8. Jackson R. Bryer, ed., *Conversations with Lillian Hellman* (Jackson: University Press of Mississippi, 1986), 115.
9. Devlin, *Conversations with Tennessee Williams*, 319.
10. Arthur Ganz, *Realms of the Self* (New York: New York University Press, 1980), 120.
11. Devlin, *Conversations with Tennessee Williams*, 318.

151

12. Ibid., 98, 137.

13. Leverich, *Tom: The Unknown Tennessee Williams*, xxiii.

CHAPTER 1. THE RISE AND FALL OF A REPUTATION

1. "'Milk Train' Gets a Second Chance," *New York Times*, 18 September 1963, 32:1. Bruce Smith mistakenly writes that "The 1963 production [of *Milk Train*] closed after five performances" (20). Smith also reports that this production was directed by Tony Richardson and starred Tallulah Bankhead and Tab Hunter. The play in fact ran on Broadway for sixty-nine performances in 1963, as the *New York Times* and Donald Spoto (285) report, and starred Hermione Baddeley and Paul Roebling (as did the Spoleto production). Smith is referring to the revised *1964* production of *Milk Train* on Broadway, which opened on 1 January 1964 and did in fact run for only five performances. It was this production that starred Tallulah Bankhead and Tab Hunter and was directed by Tony Richardson.

2. John Gassner, *The Theatre in Our Times* (New York: Crown Publishers, 1954), 359–60.

3. Ibid., 359.

4. Quoted in Robert Brustein, *Seasons of Discontent* (New York: Simon and Schuster, 1965), 282.

5. Brustein, *Seasons of Discontent*, 283.

6. Ibid.

7. Gassner, *Theatre in Our Times*, viii.

8. Strangely enough, however, in 1951 the *New York Times*, reporting on the play's opening in Hammersmith, London, called *Summer and Smoke* "Tennessee Williams' Broadway success of 1948" ("'Summer and Smoke' in London," *New York Times*, 23 November 1951, 32:7). Apparently the New York audiences and critics (such as Brooks Atkinson) who found something admirable in the play influenced its reputation somewhat, despite the play's relatively short Broadway run. In any case, the fact that *Summer and Smoke* was revived off-Broadway in 1952 (and was a great success) is an indication that the play was not an unqualified failure in New York, as was to be the fate of several of Williams' later plays.

9. Smith, *Costly Performances*, 14.

10. Donald Spoto writes that *The Rose Tattoo* opened at the Martin Beck Theatre on 3 February *1950*. This is a typographical error; both Albert J. Devlin (xvii) and Bruce Smith (13) record the date of the opening as 3 February 1951, as does the published version of *The Rose Tattoo*.

11. Quoted in Smith, *Costly Performances*, 81.

12. Claudia Cassidy, "Fragile Drama Holds Together in Tight Spell," *Chicago Daily Tribune*, 27 December 1944, 11, quoted in Spoto, *Kindness of Strangers*, 121–22.

13. Ashton Stevens, "Great Actress Proves It In Fine Way," *Chicago Herald American*, 27 December 1944, 11, quoted in Spoto, *Kindness of Strangers*, 122.

14. Lewis Nichols, *New York Times*, 2 April 1945, 15:5.

15. George Jean Nathan, *The Theatre Book of the Year 1944–45* (New York: Knopf, 1945), 326–27.

16. Brooks Atkinson, quoted in Benedict Nightingale, "This 'Menagerie' Is Much Too Cozy," *New York Times*, 11 December 1983, 2:3.

17. Smith, *Costly Performances*, 9.

18. Brooks Atkinson, "'Streetcar' Tragedy," *New York Times*, 14 December 1947, 2:3:1.

19. Brooks Atkinson, *New York Times*, 25 March 1955, 18:2.

20. Walter Kerr, *The Commonweal*, 23 February 1951, 492.

21. Walter Kerr, *New York Herald-Tribune* 8 January 1958, 16.

22. Harold Clurman, *Lies Like Truth* (New York: Macmillan, 1958), 14.

23. "The Angel of the Odd," *Time* 79 (9 March 1962): 53.

24. "Williams Drama Baffles Critics," *New York Times*, 13 December 1967, 54:5.

25. Clive Barnes, "'The Seven Descents of Myrtle' at Barrymore," *New York Times*, 28 March 1968, 54:1. *The Seven Descents of Myrtle* was revised and presented once again, under the title *Kingdom of Earth*, at the McCarter Theatre in Princeton, New Jersey, on 6 March 1975. Clive Barnes reviewed this production as well (*New York Times*, 12 March 1975, 28:1), and still maintained that the play was "not among the playwright's best," and that "the fault of the play is simply that the characters are more fully realized than their motives. The construction is flimsy."

26. Clive Barnes, "Williams Play Explores Decay of an Artist," *New York Times*, 12 May 1969, 54:1.

27. Walter Kerr, "A Touch of the Poet Isn't Enough to Sustain Williams's Latest Play," *New York Times*, 22 May 1977, 2:5:1.

28. Walter Kerr, "People Out of Books," *New York Times*, 27 March 1980, C15:1.

29. "Williams Drama Baffles Critics," *New York Times*, 13 December 1967, 54:5.

30. Lawrence Van Gelder, *New York Times*, 22 August 1975, 16:5.

31. Clive Barnes, "Williams Play Explores Decay of an Artist," *New York Times*, 12 May 1969, 54:1.

32. Quoted in Smith, *Costly Performances*, 22.

33. Richard Eder, "Bittersweet Realism," *New York Times*, 22 January 1979, C15:1.

34. C. W. E. Bigsby, *Modern American Drama, 1945–1990* (Cambridge: Cambridge University Press, 1992), 65.

35. Spoto, *Kindness of Strangers*, 321.

36. Gassner, *Theatre in Our Times*, 349.

37. Ibid.

38. Ibid., 355.

39. Ibid., 357.

40. Ibid., 358.

41. Ibid., 461.

42. Eric Bentley, *In Search of Theatre* (New York: Alfred A. Knopf, 1953), 31.

43. Ibid., 33.

44. Ibid., 34, emphasis mine.

45. Ibid., 34.

46. Eric Bentley, *The Dramatic Event* (New York: Horizon Press, 1954), 108.

47. Eric Bentley, *What Is Theatre?* (1968; reprint, New York: Limelight Editions, 1984), 231.

48. Ibid., 228.

49. Ibid., 230.

50. Ibid., 229.

51. Ibid., 227.

52. Kenneth Tynan, *Curtains* (New York: Atheneum, 1961), 72.

53. Ibid., 266.

54. Ibid., 291.

55. Ibid., 262.

56. Ibid., 270.

57. Ibid., 271.

58. Ibid., 280.

59. Ibid., 264.

60. Robert Brustein, *Critical Moments* (New York: Random House, 1980), 112.

61. Ibid., 93.

62. Robert Brustein, *Seasons of Discontent* (New York: Simon and Schuster, 1965), 126.

63. Signi Falk, "The Profitable World of Tennessee Williams," *Modern Drama* 1 (December 1958): 172.

64. Ibid., 173–74.

65. Ibid., 180.

66. Robert Emmet Jones, "Tennessee Williams' Early Heroines," *Modern Drama* 2 (December 1959): 211.

67. Brustein, *Seasons*, 129.

68. Ibid., 283.

69. Arthur Ganz, "The Desperate Morality of the Plays of Tennessee Williams," *American Scholar* 31 (spring 1962): 284.

70. Ganz, *Realms of the Self*, 119.

71. Ibid., 120–21.

72. William J. Free, "Williams in the Seventies: Directions and Discontents," in *Tennessee Williams: 13 Essays*, ed. Jac Tharpe (Jackson: University Press of Mississippi, 1980), 247.

73. Ibid., 254.

74. Smith, *Costly Performances*, 19.

75. Ibid., 18.

76. Brooks Atkinson, "Williams' 'Sweet Bird of Youth' Opens," *New York Times*, 11 March 1959, 39:2.

77. Harold Clurman, *The Nation* 188 (28 March 1959): 281–83.

78. John Chapman, *New York Daily News*, 11 March 1959, 65, quoted in Spoto, *Kindness of Strangers*, 256.

79. Smith, *Costly Performances*, 19.

80. Ibid.

81. Spoto, *Kindness of Strangers*, 254. In a footnote, Spoto points out that Williams, "beyond any link with reality . . . gave the impression that his financial situation was precarious. Meade Roberts recalled that once, in a Miami bookshop, Williams had decided to purchase a limited edition of Van Gogh's letters to his brother. But when he was told that the book cost fifty dollars, Williams reneged, saying, 'I can't afford it'" (254).

82. Quoted in Smith, *Costly Performances*, 19.

83. Spoto calls *Camino Real* an "experimental, poetic *but not obscure* play" (207, emphasis mine), and feels it has "lusty humor and a poise between politics and poetics" (208). Spoto feels that perhaps the reason *Camino* did not succeed was that "audiences in 1953 rejected the play not in fact because it was vague, but because it was all too clear in its denunciation of the fascist demagoguery then spreading over the country in the voice, especially loud, of Senator Joseph

McCarthy" (208). That explanation seems plausible when seen in light of a play which was a product of the same year as *Camino* and also failed commercially, Arthur Miller's *The Crucible*, a blatant denouncing of McCarthyism. *The Crucible* "ran for only 197 performances, towards the end being kept alive by a cast willing to work for little or no pay," yet Bigsby points out that eventually *The Crucible* was to become Miller's most popular play, transcending its relevance to McCarthyism and proving significant to other urgencies as it was performed around the world, in countries such as China and Poland (Bigsby, *Modern American Drama*, 93). *Camino Real*, however, is, in terms of form, a very different play from Miller's, and, unlike *The Crucible*, has in general never become successful with audiences, reviewers, or critics.

84. Spoto, *Kindness of Strangers*, 196.

85. Walter Kerr, "Camino Real," *New York Herald-Tribune*, 20 March 1953, 12.

86. Walter Kerr, in a letter to Tennessee Williams dated 13 April 1953, quoted in Spoto, *Kindness of Strangers*, 208–9.

87. Walter Kerr, *Pieces at Eight* (New York: Simon and Schuster, 1957), 134.

88. Smith, *Costly Performances*, 15–16.

89. Spoto, *Kindness of Strangers*, 232.

90. John Chapman, *New York Daily News*, 23 November 1956, 60, quoted in Spoto, *Kindness of Strangers*, 232.

91. Brooks Atkinson, *New York Times*, 22 November 1956, 50:1.

92. Clive Barnes, *New York Times*, 12 May 1969, 54:1.

93. Walter Kerr, in a letter to Tennessee Williams dated 13 April 1953, quoted in Spoto, *Kindness of Strangers*, 209.

94. Devlin, *Conversations with Tennessee Williams*, 240.

95. David Greggory to Donald Spoto, 12 August 1983, quoted in Spoto, *Kindness of Strangers*, 284.

96. Spoto, *Kindness of Strangers*, 372.

97. Bentley, *Dramatic Event*, 107.

98. Ibid., 110.

99. Ibid., 108.

100. Ibid.

101. Tynan, *Curtains*, 264.

102. Ibid., 266.

103. John Gassner, review of *Summer and Smoke*, *Forum* 110 (December 1948), quoted in Ronald Hayman, *Everyone Else Is an Audience* (New Haven: Yale University Press, 1993), 126.

104. Spoto, *Kindness of Strangers*, 285.

105. Tennessee Williams, *The Theatre of Tennessee Williams*, 8 vols. (New York: New Directions, 1971–92), 6:40. Unless otherwise noted, all quotations from Williams' plays will be taken from this source and cited by volume and page number in the text.

106. Devlin, *Conversations with Tennessee Williams*, 97–98.

107. Leverich, *Tom: The Unknown Tennessee Williams*, xxiii.

108. Devlin, *Conversations with Tennessee Williams*, 236.

109. Ibid., 240.

110. Ibid., 255.

111. Ibid., 319.

112. Smith, *Costly Performances*, 16.

113. Elliot Martin to Donald Spoto, 19 October 1983, quoted in Spoto, *Kindness of Strangers*, 368.

CHAPTER 2. "I DON'T LIKE TO WRITE REALISTICALLY": WILLIAMS' UNEASY RELATIONSHIP WITH REALISM

1. I shall be discussing Williams' use of nondiegetic devices in *Menagerie* and *Streetcar* more fully later in this chapter.

2. Gassner, *Theatre in Our Times*, 351.

3. Hayman, *Everyone Else Is an Audience*, 193.

4. Smith, *Costly Performances*, 15.

5. Bigsby, *Modern American Drama*, 36.

6. Benjamin Nelson, *Tennessee Williams: The Man and His Work* (New York: Ivan Obolensky, 1961), 239.

7. Joseph N. Riddel, "A Streetcar Named Desire—*Nietzche Descending*," in *Modern Critical Views: Tennessee Williams*, ed. Harold Bloom (New York: Chelsea House Publishers, 1987), 13.

8. Bentley, *In Search of Theatre*, 34.

9 M. H. Abrams, *A Glossary of Literary Terms* (Orlando: Harcourt Brace Jovanovich, 1993), 174.

10. Catherine Belsey, *Critical Practice* (New York: Methuen, 1980), 70.

11. Vivian M. Patraka, "Lillian Hellman's *Watch on the Rhine*: Realism, Gender, and Historical Crisis," *Modern Drama* 32 (March 1989): 128.

12. Elin Diamond, "Mimesis, Mimicry, and the 'True-Real,'" *Modern Drama* 32 (March 1989): 60.

13. Ian Watt, *The Rise of the Novel* (London: Chatto and Windus, 1957), 23.

14. George Levine, *The Realistic Imagination* (Chicago: University of Chicago Press, 1981), 6.

15. Phyllis Hartnoll and Peter Found, eds., *The Concise Oxford Companion to the Theatre* (New York: Oxford University Press, 1993), 409.

16. Bigsby, *Modern American Drama*, 36. When asked by Cecil Brown in 1974 if he uses the "principle of exaggeration" in his work, Williams replied: "I exaggerate because I don't like to write realistically; it doesn't interest me very much" (Devlin, *Conversations with Tennessee Williams*, 262–63). In 1973 he told C. Robert Jennings that "the critics want me to be a poetic realist, and I never was" (Devlin, *Conversations with Tennessee Williams*, 240).

17. Levine, *The Realistic Imagination*, 8.

18. Christine R. Day and Bob Woods, eds., *Where I Live: Selected Essays by Tennessee Williams* (New York: New Directions, 1978), 109–10.

19. Ibid., 91–92.

20. Émile Zola, "Naturalism in the Theatre," in *The Theory of the Modern Stage*, ed. Eric Bentley (Baltimore: Penguin Books, 1968), 362.

21. Ibid., 364.

22. Ibid., 370.

23. Ibid., 371.

24. Ibid., 370.

25. Ibid., 371.

26. Riddel, "A Streetcar Named Desire," 13.

27. Kazan, *A Life*, 330.

28. Gassner, *Theatre in Our Times*, 351.

29. Ibid., 350.

30. Ibid., 351.

31. Roger Boxill, *Tennessee Williams* (London: Macmillan, 1988), 28.

32. Devlin, *Conversations with Tennessee Williams*, 125.

33. David Savran, *Communists, Cowboys, and Queers: The Politics of Masculinity in the Works of Arthur Miller and Tennessee Williams* (Minneapolis: University of Minnesota Press, 1992), 93.

34. Ibid.

35. Ibid.

36. Ibid., 92.

37. Ibid., 92–93.

38. Ibid., 92.

39. Williams' early one-act play, *The Purification* (1945), which is written in verse, and *Camino Real* are the only radical departures from the essentially realistic plays of his early period.

40. Devlin, *Conversations with Tennessee Williams*, 329.

41. Ibid., 85.

42. Thornton Wilder, *Our Town*, in *Three Plays* (New York: Harper, 1957), 70. Hereafter cited by page number in the text.

43. Wilder, "Preface," in *Three Plays*, xi–xii.

44. See, for example, Caryl Churchill's *Top Girls* (1982, 1984, 1990).

45. Nelson, *Tennessee Williams*, 239.

46. Kazan, *A Life*, 541.

47. Ibid., 542–43.

48. Ibid., 541–42.

49. Ibid., 542–43.

50. Quoted in Rader, *Tennessee: Cry of the Heart*, 166–67.

51. Levine, *The Realistic Imagination*, 12.

52. Ibid., 8.

53. Ibid.

54. Belsey, *Critical Practice*, 67.

55. Bigsby, *Modern American Drama*, 72.

56. James Reynolds, "The Failure of Technology in *The Glass Menagerie*," *Modern Drama* 34 (December 1991): 522.

57. Ibid., 522–23.

58. Riddel, "A Streetcar Named Desire," 13.

59. Esther Merle Jackson, "The Synthetic Myth," in Bloom, *Modern Critical Views: Tennessee Williams*, ed. Harold Bloom (New York: Chelsea House, 1987), 26.

60. Reynolds, "The Failure of Technology," 525.

61. Grigor Pavlov, quoted in Reynolds, "The Failure of Technology," 526.

62. Riddel, "A Streetcar Named Desire," 19.

63. Alvin B. Kernan, "Truth and Dramatic Mode in *A Streetcar Named Desire*," in *Modern Critical Views: Tennessee Williams*, ed. Harold Bloom (New York: Chelsea House, 1987), 9.

64. Harry Taylor, "The Dilemma of Tennessee Williams," *Massess and Mainstream* 1 (1948): 54.

65. Ibid.

66. Ibid.

67. George Niesen, "The Artist against the Reality in the Plays of Tennessee Williams," in *Tennessee Williams: 13 Essays*, ed. Jac Tharpe (Jackson: University Press of Mississippi, 1980), 82.

68. Taylor, "The Dilemma of Tennessee Williams," 55.

69. Devlin, *Conversations with Tennessee Williams*, 277.

70. Taylor, "The Dilemma of Tennessee Williams," 55.

71. Tennessee Williams, *Baby Doll*, 1956. Produced and directed in winter 1955–56 by Elia Kazan for Newtown Productions, Inc., and released by Warner Brothers. The principal roles are filled by Carroll Baker, Eli Wallach, Karl Malden, and Mildred Dunnock. All references to *Baby Doll* are taken directly from the filmed version, as the published version of the "shooting" script made available by New Directions (New York, 1956) differs slightly from the version released to the public.

CHAPTER 3. THE FUSION OF PUN AND POETRY: A MOVEMENT TOWARD "FREER FORMS"

1. Devlin, *Conversations with Tennessee Williams*, 98.

2. Ibid., 218.

3. Michael Vanden Heuvel, *Performing Drama/Dramatizing Performance* (Ann Arbor: University of Michigan Press, 1991), 28.

4. Devlin, *Conversations with Tennessee Williams*, 99.

5. Ibid., 118.

6. Ibid., 98.

7. Ibid.

8. Tennessee Williams, introduction to Carson McCullers, *Reflections in a Golden Eye* (New York: Bantam Books, 1967), x.

9. *transition* (1949):98.

10. Devlin, *Conversations with Tennessee Williams*, 99.

11. Bigsby, *Modern American Drama*, 241.

12. Devlin, *Conversations with Tennessee Williams*, 255.

13. Ibid., 234.

14. Tennessee Williams, *Memoirs* (New York: Doubleday and Company, 1975), 187.

15. Devlin, *Conversations with Tennessee Williams*, 136.

16. Spoto, *Kindness of Strangers*, 389–90.

17. Tennessee Williams, introduction to McCullers, *Reflections in a Golden Eye*, xiii.

18. Devlin, *Conversations with Tennessee Williams*, 293.

19. Ibid.

20. Ibid., 294.

21. Richard Christiansen, "At 70, Even Tennessee Williams is Impressed," *New York Daily News*, 23 April 1981, 41, quoted in Spoto, *Kindness of Strangers*, 305.

22. Maureen Stapleton to Donald Spoto, 16 January 1984, quoted in Spoto, *Kindness of Strangers*, 293.

23. Devlin, *Conversations with Tennessee Williams*, 294.

24. Day and Woods, *Where I Live*, 25.

25. Devlin, *Conversations with Tennessee Williams*, 294.

26. This latest version (published 1976) in volume 5 of *The Theatre of Tennessee Williams* is the one I will be quoting from throughout my text, unless otherwise noted.

27. Devlin, *Conversations with Tennessee Williams*, 239.

28. Maria St. Just, *Five O'Clock Angel* (New York: Alfred A. Knopf, 1990), 195.

29. Boxill, *Tennessee Williams*, 149.

30. Dakin Williams and Shepard Mead, *Tennessee Williams: An Intimate Biography* (New York: Arbor House, 1983), 270.

31. Devlin, *Conversations with Tennessee Williams*, 255.

32. Bigsby, *Modern American Drama*, 138.

33. Devlin, *Conversations with Tennessee Williams*, 185.

34. Bigsby, *Modern American Drama*, 28.

35. Ibid., 67.

36. Moreover, in the first quoted passage it is the characters' "house" which becomes a prison, whereas later, in the second, it the "theater" which undergoes this transformation. And even though in this case Clare and Felice use the term "house" in a relatively literal sense to refer to a structure constituting a common living area (or its representation onstage), it is a term which can also be used to describe theater space (e.g., "The house is full tonight"). The boundaries between house/theater/prison are blurred at several levels in this play so that space is presented as both metonymically and metaphorically unstable.

37. Boxill, *Tennessee Williams*, 151.

38. Bigsby, *Modern American Drama*, 67.

39. C. W. E. Bigsby, "Valedictory," in *Modern Critical Views: Tennessee Williams*, ed. Harold Bloom (New York: Chelsea House, 1987), 133.

40. Tennessee Williams, *Out Cry* (New York: New Directions, 1973), 9.

41. See chapter 2.

42. Michel Foucault, "The Discourse on Language," in *The Archaeology of Knowledge and The Discourse on Language*, trans. A. M. Sheridan Smith (New York: Pantheon, 1972), 222.

43. Ibid., 217.

44. Williams and Mead, *Tennessee Williams*, 270.

45. Devlin, *Conversations with Tennessee Williams*, 239.

46. Leverich, *Tom: The Unknown Tennessee Williams*, 9.

47. Elia Kazan to Donald Spoto, 1 February 1984, quoted in Spoto, *Kindness of Strangers*, 316.

48. While Williams scholarship has, until now, documented Rose's infamous lobotomy as having taken place in August or September 1937, new evidence by Lyle Leverich in his biography *Tom: The Unknown Tennessee Williams* locates the operation six years later. Leverich writes that a letter dated 7 August 1937 from Williams' paternal aunt, Isabel Williams Brownlow, to his father referring to a "treatment" for Rose

> has often been misconstrued to mean the treatment was a prefrontal lobotomy, when is fact Isabel Brownlow was referring to insulin shock therapy and was approving the move to Farmington State Hospital for that purpose. Whether Edwina [Williams' mother] intended to mislead readers of her memoir in order to place the ultimate responsibility on her husband or whether she misinterpreted the content of Isabel's letter can only be left to conjecture. The lobotomy did not actually take place until six years later, under very different circumstances. Not only Edwina but also Tennessee, unwittingly or not, perpetuated the fiction that the operation was performed in August or September of 1937, when even medically this was an impossibility. (225)

49. The *Washington Post* (10 September 1996, B: 5:1) reports that Rose Williams died at age eighty-six on 4 September 1996 of cardiac arrest. This seems to be the most accurate obituary, as I found several inconsistencies. The *New*

York Times (7 September 1996, A: 13: 4), for example, erroneously reports the date of her death as 5 September, while the *Los Angeles Times* (7 September 1996, A: 20: 1) states Rose's age as eighty-seven. Since Rose was born in November, she died before her eighty-seventh birthday. The funeral was held on 9 September 1996 in Clayton, Missouri (*St-Louis Post-Dispatch*, 8 September 1996, D: 11: 3).

50. Williams, *Memoirs*, 221.

51. Boxill, *Tennessee Williams*, 22.

52. *People* interview, 7 May 1979, 34, quoted in Spoto, *Kindness of Strangers*, 373.

53. Quoted in Williams and Mead, *Tennessee Williams*, 271.

54. Day and Woods, *Where I Live*, 125.

55. Niesen, "The Artist against the Reality," 81.

56. Devlin, *Conversations with Tennessee Williams*, 239.

57. Hayman, *Everyone Else Is an Audience*, 203.

58. Norman J. Fedder, "Tennessee Williams' Dramatic Technique," in *Tennessee Williams: 13 Essays*, ed. Jac Tharpe (Jackson: University Press of Mississippi, 1980), 244.

59. William Leonard, review of *Out Cry*, *Chicago Tribune*, 9 July 1971, quoted in Hayman, *Everyone Else Is an Audience*, 213.

60. Ganz, *Realms of the Self*, 120.

61. Ibid.

62. Ibid.

63. Peggy W. Prenshaw, "The Paradoxical Southern World of Tennessee Williams," in *Tennessee Williams: 13 Essays*, ed. Jac Tharpe (Jackson: University Press of Mississippi, 1980), 15.

64. Niesen, "The Artist against the Reality," 83.

65. Charles B. Brooks, "Williams' Comedy," in *Tennessee Williams: 13 Essays*, ed. Jac Tharpe (Jackson: University Press of Mississippi, 1980), 185.

66. Leverich, *Tom: The Unknown Tennessee Williams*, xxiii.

67. Devlin, *Conversations with Tennessee Williams*, 218.

Chapter 4. Weak Dramatic Experiments and the Reluctant Return to Realism

1. Devlin, *Conversations with Tennessee Williams*, 287. For comments on Williams' sense that he was losing command over the theater, see Devlin, *Conversations with Tennessee Williams*, 285–86.

2. Ibid., 286.

3. Ibid., 108.

4. Ibid., 286.

5. Boxill, *Tennessee Williams*, 146.

6. Hayman, *Everyone Else Is an Audience*, 193.

7. Robert Bechtold Heilman, "The Middle Years," in *Modern Critical Views: Tennessee Williams*, ed. Harold Bloom (New York: Chelsea House, 1987), 82.

8. Boxill, *Tennessee Williams*, 146.

9. Spoto, *Kindness of Strangers*, 289.

10. Devlin, *Conversations with Tennessee Williams*, 196.

11. Hayman, *Everyone Else Is an Audience*, 194.

12. Devlin, *Conversations with Tennessee Williams*, 211.

13. Ibid., 196.

14. Ibid., 285.

15. Hayman, *Everyone Else Is an Audience*, 221.

16. Devlin, *Conversations with Tennessee Williams*, 274.

17. Boxill, *Tennessee Williams*, 157.

18. Devlin, *Conversations with Tennessee Williams*, 291.

19. Hayman, *Everyone Else Is an Audience*, 221.

20. Ibid.

21. Spoto, *Kindness of Strangers*, 346.

22. Devlin, *Conversations with Tennessee Williams*, 298.

23. Ibid., 291–92.

24. Ibid., 292.

25. Spoto, *Kindness of Strangers*, 347.

26. Devlin, *Conversations with Tennessee Williams*, 298.

27. Ibid., 300.

28. Walter Kerr, "A Touch of the Poet Isn't Enough to Sustain Williams's Latest Play," *New York Times*, 22 May 1977, 2:5:1.

29. Spoto, *Kindness of Strangers*, 364.

30. Ibid., 363.

31. Ibid., 364.

32. Tennessee Williams, "The Angel in the Alcove," in *Collected Stories* (New York: Ballantine Books, 1985), 131.

33. Devlin, *Conversations with Tennessee Williams*, 301.

34. Ibid.

35. Boxill, *Tennessee Williams*, 158.

36. Ibid., 159.

37. Spoto, *Kindness of Strangers*, 372.

38. Ibid.

39. John Calendo, "Tennessee Talks to John Calendo," *Interview* (April 1973): 28, quoted in Spoto, *Kindness of Strangers*, 289.

40. Day and Woods, *Where I Live*, 157–58.

41. Ibid., 159.

42. Boxill, *Tennessee Williams*, 164.

43. Michiko Kakutani, "Tennessee Williams: 'I Keep Writing: Sometimes I Am Pleased'," *New York Times*, 13 August 1981, C17.

44. Boxill, *Tennessee Williams*, 164.

45. Spoto, *Kindness of Strangers*, 396.

46. Boxill, *Tennessee Williams*, 165.

Chapter 5. Critical Expectations and Assumptions: Williams' Later Reputation and the American Reception of the Avant-Garde

1. Devlin, *Conversations with Tennessee Williams*, 284–85.

2. Ibid., 98, 137.

3. *Waiting for Godot*, however, was not performed in the United States until 1956.

4. James Coakley, "Time and Tide on the *Camino Real*," in Bloom, *Modern Critical Views: Tennessee Williams* (New York: Chelsea House, 1987), 98.

5. Niesen, "The Artist against the Reality," 106.

6. Ibid., 107.

7. Bigsby, "Valedictory," 132–33.

8. Samuel Beckett, *Molloy, Malone Dies, The Unnamable* (New York: Grove Press, 1955), 18.

9. Samuel Beckett, *Waiting For Godot* (New York: Grove Press, 1954), 9.

10. Ibid., 12.

11. Samuel Beckett, *Endgame* (New York: Grove Press, 1958), 58.

12. Vanden Heuvel, *Performing Drama/Dramatizing Performance*, 90.

13. Beckett, *Endgame*, 44.

14. Ibid., 81.

15. Ibid., 79.

16. Beckett, *Molloy, Malone Dies, The Unnamable*, 302.

17. Ibid., 291.

18. Ibid., 414.

19. Warren Lee, "The Bitter Pill of Samuel Beckett," *Chicago Review* 10:4 (1957): 79.

20. Ibid., 79–80.

21. Ibid., 77.

22. Ibid., 78.

23. Ibid.

24. Ibid.

25. Ibid., 79.

26. Clurman, *Lies Like Truth*, 15.

27. Bentley, *What Is Theatre?*, 297.

28. Tynan, *Curtains*, 272.

29. A. J. Leventhal, "Samuel Beckett, Poet and Pessimist," *The Listener* 57 (9 May 1957): 747.

30. Quoted in Bentley, *What Is Theatre?*, 298.

31. Ibid., 297.

32. W. A. Darlington, *New York Times*, 13 November 1955, 2:3:1.

33. Brooks Atkinson, *New York Times*, 20 April 1956, 21:2.

34. Tynan, *Curtains*, 101.

35. Martin Esslin, *The Theatre of the Absurd* (1961; reprint, New York: Penguin Books, 1980), 40.

36. Tynan, *Curtains*, 272.

37. Brooks Atkinson, *New York Times*, 30 January 1958, 18:3.

38. Lewis Funke, *New York Times*, 12 February 1962, 27:1.

39. Walter Kerr, *Thirty Days Hath November* (New York: Simon and Schuster, 1969), 41.

40. Howard Taubman, *New York Times*, 5 October 1961, 42:3.

41. B. A. Young, *New York Times*, 4 June 1965, 38:8.

42. Kerr, *Thirty Days Hath November*, 45.

43. Brooks Atkinson, *New York Times*, 16 February 1958, 2:1:1.

44. Brooks Atkinson, *New York Times*, 29 April 1956, 2:1:2.

45. John Gassner, *Dramatic Soundings* (New York: Crown Publishers, 1968), 113.

46. Ibid., 692.

47. Ibid., 503.

48. Bentley, *What Is Theatre?*, 301.

49. Eric Bentley, *The Life of the Drama* (New York: Atheneum, 1964), 100–101.

50. Robert Brustein, *The Theatre of Revolt* (Boston: Little, Brown, and Company, 1964), 377.

51. Kenneth Rexroth, "The Point Is Irrelevance," *The Nation* (14 April 1956): 325.

52. Tynan, *Curtains*, 103.

53. Ibid., 101.

54. Edith Kern, "Drama Stripped for Inaction: Beckett's *Godot*," *Yale French Studies* 14 (1955): 45.

55. Ibid., 41–42.

56. Ibid., 47.

57. Gassner, *Dramatic Soundings*, 506–7.

58. Arthur Ganz, "Mixing Memory and Desire: Pinter's Vision in *Landscape, Silence,* and *Old Times*," in *Pinter: A Collection of Critical Essays*, ed. Arthur Ganz (Englewood Cliffs, N.J.: Prentice Hall, 1972), 177–78.

59. Gassner, *Dramatic Soundings*, 692.

60. Ibid., 503.

61. Bentley, *The Life of the Drama*, 101.

62. Tynan, *Curtains*, 101.

63. John E. Booth, *The Critic, Power, and the Performing Arts* (New York: Columbia University Press, 1992), 116.

64. Spoto, *Kindness of Strangers*, 297.

65. Vassilis Voglis to Donald Spoto, 22 September 1983, quoted in Spoto, *Kindness of Strangers*, 297.

Select Bibliography

Abrams, M. H. *A Glossary of Literary Terms*. Orlando: Harcourt Brace Jovanovich, 1993.

Beckett, Samuel. *Endgame*. New York: Grove Press, 1958

———. *Molloy, Malone Dies, The Unnamable*. New York: Grove Press, 1955.

———. *Waiting For Godot*. New York: Grove Press, 1954.

Belsey, Catherine. *Critical Practice*. New York: Methuen, 1980.

Bentley, Eric. *The Dramatic Event*. New York: Horizon Press, 1954.

———. *In Search of Theatre*. New York: Alfred A. Knopf, 1953.

———. *The Life of the Drama*. New York: Atheneum, 1964.

———, ed. *The Theory of the Modern Stage*. Baltimore: Penguin Books, 1968.

———. *What Is Theatre?* 1968. Reprint, New York: Limelight Editions, 1984.

Bigsby, C. W. E. "Valedictory." In *Modern Critical Views: Tennessee Williams*, edited by Harold Bloom, 131–49. New York: Chelsea House, 1987.

———. *Modern American Drama, 1945–1990*. Cambridge: Cambridge University Press, 1992.

Bloom, Harold, ed. *Modern Critical Views: Tennessee Williams*. New York: Chelsea House, 1987.

Booth, John E. *The Critic, Power, and the Performing Arts*. New York: Columbia University Press, 1992.

Boxill, Roger. *Tennessee Williams*. London: Macmillan, 1988.

Brooks, Charles B. "Williams' Comedy." In *Tennessee Williams: 13 Essays*, edited by Jac Tharpe, 173–88. Jackson: University Press of Mississippi, 1980.

Brustein, Robert. *Critical Moments*. New York: Random House, 1980.

———. *Seasons of Discontent*. New York: Simon and Schuster, 1965.

———. *The Theatre of Revolt*. Boston: Little, Brown, and Company, 1964.

Bryer, Jackson R., ed. *Conversations with Lillian Hellman*. Jackson: University Press of Mississippi, 1986.

Clurman, Harold. *The Collected Works of Harold Clurman*. Edited by Marjorie Leggatt and Glenn Young. New York: Applause Books, 1954.

———. *Lies Like Truth*. New York: Macmillan, 1958.

Coakley, James. "Time and Tide on the *Camino Real*." In *Modern Critical Views: Tennessee Williams*, edited by Harold Bloom, 95–98. New York: Chelsea House, 1987.

Devlin, Albert J., ed. *Conversations with Tennessee Williams*. Jackson: University Press of Mississippi, 1986.

Diamond, Elin. "Mimesis, Mimicry, and the "True-Real." *Modern Drama* 32 (March 1989): 58–72.

Dickens, Charles. *David Copperfield*. 1850. Reprint, Oxford: Oxford University Press, 1991.

Esslin, Martin. *The Theatre of the Absurd*. 1961. Reprint, New York: Penguin Books, 1980.

Falk, Signi. "The Profitable World of Tennessee Williams." *Modern Drama* 1 (December 1958): 172–80.

———. *Tennessee Williams*. New York: Twayne Publishers, 1961.

Fedder, Norman J. "Tennessee Williams' Dramatic Technique." In *Tennessee Williams: 13 Essays*, edited by Jac Tharpe, 229–46. Jackson: University Press of Mississippi, 1980.

Foucault, Michel. *The Archaeology of Knowledge and The Discourse on Language*, translated by A. M. Sheridan Smith. New York: Pantheon, 1972.

Free, William J. "Williams in the Seventies: Directions and Discontents." In *Tennessee Williams: 13 Essays*, edited by Jac Tharpe, 247–60. Jackson: University Press of Mississippi, 1980.

Ganz, Arthur. "The Desperate Morality of The Plays of Tennessee Williams." *American Scholar* 31 (spring 1962): 278–94.

———. "Mixing Memory and Desire: Pinter's Vision in *Landscape, Silence*, and *Old Times*." In *Pinter: A Collection of Critical Essays*, edited by Arthur Ganz, 161–78. Englewood Cliffs, N.J.: Prentice Hall, 1972.

———. *Realms of the Self*. New York: New York University Press, 1980.

Gassner, John. *Dramatic Soundings*. New York: Crown Publishers, 1968.

———. *The Theatre in Our Times*. New York: Crown Publishers, 1954.

Hartnoll, Phyllis, and Peter Found, eds. *The Concise Oxford Companion to the Theatre*. New York: Oxford University Press, 1993.

Hayman, Ronald. *Everyone Else Is an Audience*. New Haven: Yale University Press, 1993.

Heilman, Robert Bechtold. "The Middle Years." In *Modern Critical Views: Tennessee Williams*, edited by Harold Bloom, 71–83. New York: Chelsea House, 1987.

Jackson, Esther Merle. "The Synthetic Myth." In *Modern Critical Views: Tennessee Williams*, edited by Harold Bloom, 23–42. New York: Chelsea House, 1987.

Jones, Robert Emmet. "Tennessee Williams' Early Heroines." *Modern Drama* 2 (December 1959): 211–19.

Kazan, Elia. *Elia Kazan: A Life*. New York: Doubleday, 1988.

Kern, Edith. "Drama Stripped for Inaction: Beckett's *Godot*." *Yale French Studies* 14 (1955): 41–47.

Kernan, Alvin B. "Truth and Dramatic Mode in *A Streetcar Named Desire*." In *Modern Critical Views: Tennessee Williams*, edited by Harold Bloom, 9–11. New York: Chelsea House, 1987.

Kerr, Walter. *Pieces at Eight*. New York: Simon and Schuster, 1957.

———. "The Rose Tattoo." *The Commonweal* 53 (23 February 1951): 492–93.

———. *Thirty Days Hath November*. New York: Simon and Schuster, 1969.

Lee, Warren. "The Bitter Pill of Samuel Beckett." *Chicago Review* 10:4 (1957): 77–87.

Leventhal, A. J. "Samuel Beckett, Poet and Pessimist." *The Listener* 57 (9 May 1957): 746–47.

Leverich, Lyle. *Tom: The Unknown Tennessee Williams.* New York: Crown, 1995.

Levine, George. *The Realistic Imagination.* Chicago: University of Chicago Press, 1981.

Nathan, George Jean. *The Theatre Book of the Year 1944–45.* New York: Alfred A. Knopf, 1945.

Nelson, Benjamin. *Tennessee Williams: The Man and His Work.* New York: Ivan Obolensky, 1961.

Niesen, George. "The Artist against the Reality in the Plays of Tennessee Williams." In *Tennessee Williams: 13 Essays,* edited by Jac Tharpe, 81–111. Jackson: University Press of Mississippi, 1980.

Patraka, Vivian M. "Lillian Hellman's *Watch on the Rhine:* Realism, Gender, and Historical Crisis." *Modern Drama* 32 (March 1989): 128–45.

Prenshaw, Peggy W. "The Paradoxical Southern World of Tennessee Williams." In *Tennessee Williams: 13 Essays,* edited by Jac Tharpe, 3–27. Jackson: University Press of Mississippi, 1980.

Rader, Dotson. *Tennessee: Cry of the Heart.* New York: Doubleday, 1985.

Rexroth, Kenneth. "The Point is Irrelevance." *The Nation* (14 April 1956): 325–28.

Reynolds, James. "The Failure of Technology in *The Glass Menagerie.*" *Modern Drama* 34 (December 1991): 522-27.

Riddel, Joseph N. "A Streetcar Named Desire—*Nietzche Descending.*" In *Modern Critical Views: Tennessee Williams,* edited by Harold Bloom, 13–22. New York: Chelsea House, 1987.

Savran, David. *Communists, Cowboys, and Queers: The Politics of Masculinity in the Works of Arthur Miller and Tennessee Williams.* Minneapolis: University of Minnesota Press, 1992.

Smith, Bruce. *Costly Performances: Tennessee Williams: The Last Stage.* New York: Paragon House, 1990.

Spoto, Donald. *The Kindness of Strangers: The Life of Tennessee Williams.* New York: Ballantine Books, 1985.

St. Just, Maria. *Five O'Clock Angel.* New York: Alfred A. Knopf, 1990.

Taylor, Harry. "The Dilemma of Tennessee Williams." *Masses and Mainstream* 1 (1948): 51–56.

Tharpe, Jac, ed. *Tennessee Williams: 13 Essays.* Jackson: University Press of Mississippi, 1980.

Tynan, Kenneth. *Curtains.* New York: Atheneum, 1961.

Vanden Heuvel, Michael. *Performing Drama/Dramatizing Performance.* Ann Arbor: University of Michigan Press, 1991.

Watt, Ian. *The Rise of the Novel.* London: Chatto and Windus, 1957.

Wilder, Thornton. *Three Plays.* New York: Harper and Brothers, 1957.

Williams, Dakin and Shepard Mead. *Tennessee Williams: An Intimate Biography.* New York: Arbor House, 1983.

Williams, Tennessee. *Collected Stories.* New York: Ballantine Books, 1985.

———. *Memoirs.* New York: Doubleday and Company, 1975.

———. *Out Cry.* New York: New Directions, 1973.

———. Introduction to Carson McCullers' *Reflections in a Golden Eye.* New York: Bantam Books, 1967.

————. *The Theatre of Tennessee Williams.* 8 vols. New York: New Directions, 1971–92.

————. *Where I Live: Selected Essays by Tennessee Williams.* Edited by Christine R. Day and Bob Woods. New York: New Directions, 1978.

Zola, Émile. "Naturalism in the Theatre." 1881. Reprinted in *The Theory of the Modern Stage*, edited by Eric Bentley, 315–72. New York: Alfred A. Knopf, 1953.

Index